TEACH YOUR (
THE VALUE OF 1

A PROVEN SUCCESS GUIDE TO HELP PARENTS MOTIVATE CHILDREN INTO SUCCESSFUL FUTURES.

YOU WILL DISCOVER

- Success Teaching Through Short Talks
- Discovering Your Child's Hot Buttons As Effective Teaching Events
- The Innovative Use Of Visual Tours
- Teaching Money Mechanics With Show And Tell

ACTION STEPS THAT GET RESULTS

- Motivating With The Three Part Allowance
- Improve Relationships By The Power Of Family Responsibilities
- Master Self-esteem Through Extra Income Opportunities
- Recognize Powerful Danger Signs . . . And How To Avoid Being Trapped

PLUS

- Compounding Magic • Dimensions In Charity
- Success Savings • Checklists • Dozens Of Exciting Ideas
- And Much More

Teach
Your Child
The Value
Of
Money

by
HAROLD and SANDY MOE

HARSAND FINANCIAL PRESS • WISCONSIN

TEACH YOUR CHILD THE VALUE OF MONEY

HARSAND FINANCIAL PRESS
N8565 Holseth Road
P.O. Box 515
Holmen, Wisconsin 54636

PRINTED IN THE UNITED STATES OF AMERICA
ISBN 0-9612310-4-1

*To Kari and Rolf
who have taught us more
than we've taught them.*

"If I were asked what single qualification was necessary for one who has the care of children, I should say patience. Patience with their tempers, with their understandings, with their progress. Patience to go over first principles again and again, steadily to add a little every day."

....Fenelon

TABLE OF CONTENTS

INTRODUCTION

If We Don't Start Now . . . When?

In sports they talk about the "thrill of victory" and the "agony of defeat." These same phrases apply to raising children. The exquisite joy of the birth of a healthy baby is followed by postpartum depression, teething, and the terrible two's.

All parents soon learn to view the growth and development of their child as a long term commitment. The golden days of childhood, when children begin exploring their world and gaining new skills daily, are moments to treasure. The flip side of all this is the sleepless nights when a child is ill and the pain we parents feel when our child is emotionally hurt, having difficulty in school, or parting from the family at adolescence.

Years spent teaching a child about the world in which we live present a real challenge to the love, strength and patience of every parent. More than ever before, today's parents (and single parents in particular) are faced with the total responsibility of raising their children. The luxury of time is often sacrificed and cut short with no time left for yourself . . . with no sounding board for your own ideas and parental concerns . . . you just plow ahead.

Often the struggle to survive emotionally and economically interferes with a parent's own expectation of what a family should be. The difference in what children learn and experience usually depends on the commitment the parents are able to make in teaching the family's values.

There are plenty of values at work in today's society. Many of them are not what we want our children to learn. Each family — made up of at least one adult and one child — has to decide which values they will live by and which they will reject. As our children grow older, we expect them to internalize our family values . . . such as sportsmanship, honesty, responsibility, and acceptance of the importance of their education.

So when is the right time to "teach your child the value of money?" Anytime . . . now! Obviously with children you need to "start where they're at." We can't mess with Mother Nature or Father Time. It is never too early or too late. All that's needed is the desire to begin.

This book has been designed to help you. Because we are parents and have struggled (we've earned every grey hair), we have some ideas to share. Some have worked well for us; some are good ideas we've gathered through research and talking with other parents. Some ideas will work for you and your child — feel free to pick and choose the ones you are comfortable with based on your own values and situation.

How should you start? After you have read this book, discuss the ideas presented with your spouse and children. Each family is unique and situations vary. The child's allowance, family responsibilities, and extra income opportunities all depend on each family's circumstances. Each family must devote the time and energy to implement their own plan based on what is right for them. Taking the time is really important . . . along with the desire to get to know your child better and a spirit of adventure. Good luck and enjoy your journey!

"Whatever you do or dream you can, begin it. Boldness has genius, power, and magic in it."

....Goethe

CHAPTER ONE

Kids Are Complicated: "The Way It Was"

MOM & DAD

"They were the best of times. They were the worst of times. They were the days of my youth." I don't know who first made that statement, but he certainly knew what he was talking about.

Whenever I look back, I remember the way things used to be — carefree summers when I would run barefoot through the pastures on our farm in western Wisconsin. It was all simpler then. My bicycle and a dog named Prince were my best friends.

Mom always had plenty to eat. Sometimes it took a little hunting to find the chocolate cake, but it was always hidden somewhere in the closet. When I felt down, she always knew just what to say and there was never a question she couldn't answer. Today some of the answers don't fit, but that's OK.

Dad had the heavy advice and a matching hand when I needed either. But, he always had an extra dime, and it would buy about anything I could imagine. Those were the best of times.

I can still remember myself promising any deity that would listen how I would faithfully brush my teeth from this day forth, if only I could escape the dentist without a cavity . . . just this once, please!

I remember peeking into my report card envelope to get a preview of parental reaction. Oh, that hollow feeling. And high school gym class meant learning to dance . . . with a girl. My hands were cold and sweaty, no matter what I tried. Those were the worst of times.

Times have changed. As I look around at my children's world I see confusion and hear loud music. Their world is filled with pressures and stress that I never knew when I was their age. So much more is expected of them at such a young age. So many demands. So many expectations.

But, that's the way it is. I can't take my children back to the days of my youth any more than I might want to go back. I, for one, prefer today's dentists. It's not so much that another time would be better. It might have been simpler then, but that's because we were children. Today, we feel the awesome responsibility of being a parent. Nobody prepared us for that, and I never thought about asking. Mom and Dad did the very best they could with what they had. It might not have been what they would do again, but they did the best they knew how. Was it easier for them? Maybe.

Today, my children love to hear stories of when I was their age — the things I did, the trouble I found myself in, the tree forts, the clubs, and my great expeditions. Through all of this, they gain a perspective of who they are and where they came from. That's important.

Just as I have a problem comprehending my children's world, it was difficult for my parents to see and accept the world I chose. They raised me, along with four other brothers and a sister on the farm my grandfather homesteaded. For my father, this was the only life he knew. As Grandad got older, Dad was expected to take over the family farm and care for him in his old age. That's the way things were done.

For me, those days were my "good old days." Sundays were for church, visiting relatives, and picnics. It wasn't high finance and economic struggle. Anything was possible. With six children it had to be. I am happy to have lived those days, but don't send me back.

Mom taught school while Dad ran our 160 acre farm. He could relate to the land and recognized the price it required of him. He knew there had to be an easier way to live. He always suggested we look for it. Each of us took his advice and left the farm.

It's hard for any parent to imagine the life their children choose. When I chose aviation, the price for learning to fly must have given my father pause. All the licenses and ratings cost more than he had invested in his farm, which produced a living for over 50 years. And what did I have to show for it? Pieces of paper to be carried in my wallet.

I remember Mom's reaction one winter morning when I called to tell her where I was flying off to. She responded, "You shouldn't go flying today, the roads are much too slippery." It was as hard for them to see my new world as it is for me to imagine my children's.

About ten years ago, Sandy and I purchased several acres of wooded land to build our home. It had everything we were looking for . . . seclusion, woods with all kinds of wildlife, hills for hiking, and a beautiful location for our home. When Dad saw it he became visibly agitated, to think I would spend good money on land that couldn't be farmed. It was too steep and had too many trees. At best it was only good for pasture and that's what you do with land that's not good for anything. It wasn't easy for him.

When Dad died a few years ago, I realized it had become my turn to always be there. Dad was always there for me for as long as I could remember, and now it was my turn to be there for my children.

Looking back can help us see the answers to some of the problems we face today. Most importantly, our parents probably had a much harder time understanding our world than we will have comprehending our children's. Hey, think about our grandparents who went from horse and wagon to motor cars, while their children (our parents) went from steam engines to jet planes. And where are our kids headed? What an adventure awaits them!

Here is where the idea for this book began — looking back and seeing how my life started in an entirely different world than that of my children. While presenting my Personal Finance Workshops, I was impressed with the number of people who, while talking with me, would comment, "If only our children could hear this." These workshops are not for children. They are intended for people who have an income and want to make the most of it.

It would be too easy to remind everyone that **we** are the example for our children. There is much to be said for that idea, but it's only partly true because when we grew up the world operated much differently. Today's economy requires the wise use of money and a detailed understanding of the rules of the game of economics. That's why more and more people are attending workshops on money. And, since schools don't teach our children how to make their considerable spending power ($35 billion last year) work to their best interests, it's up to us, as parents, to teach them how to manage their money. Sound like a difficult task? It is; but, with a little help, it's possible. That's what this book is intended to provide. To be sure, my first book, *Make Your Paycheck Last*, is intended for those who have incomes. *Teach Your Child The Value Of Money* is intended as a guide to help teach young people the basics of money management. It's not meant for the children to study on their own. Rather, it's a tool to be used by people who influence children. Not that you must be parents by any means. You may be a teacher, grandparent, step parent, aunt, or uncle or simply a friend of a young person with questions on how to deal with money. For continuity in my commentary, I am assuming that most readers are parents. However, I have made every effort to structure this book in such a way that it is a valid tool for anyone. In many ways, the best examples (role models) for young people are those who simply care.

As you read my ideas, understand that you don't need to buy into everything I say. In some cases, ideas may not apply to your situation while others will. Once you have read the material, think about your situation and use the ideas you agree with. There are many ways to teach.

In the course of preparing this book, I interviewed people from every region of this country. That was one of the rewards of this undertaking — talking to so many people with "hands on" experience and years of know how from all backgrounds and persuasions. None summed up your task better than a friend I met in Boston. He said, "There are only two things as complicated as raising kids, and I have no idea what they are."

CHAPTER TWO

A Parent Conflict: "Examining Yourself"

Today's world is a world of apparent conflict. This is never clearer than when we listen to our children and observe the social values they reflect. As parents raised in another generation, we see contradicting values between us and our children. Here is what I mean.

Our parents grew up in the Depression era. The traditional value that grew out of that time was, "Waste not, want not." Don't waste anything. Mend a torn knee. Eat everything on your plate — there are starving children in China. Save today so you will have something for tomorrow. These are the values they sold us.

Today, we're called the throw-away society. "Buy now and pay later." Fast and instant everything. Why keep the old when the new is so much better? Don't wait, why put it off any longer? This offer may never be repeated. These are the values being sold to our children today.

Here is where much of the conflict is rooted. Parents of today still buy into much of what their parents valued and lived. That is true to a varying degree with everyone. The work ethic of "work hard and anything is possible" is still believable today. The Great

American Dream! It says you can achieve anything you want, just get out there and do it. Go for the brass ring.

The problem seems to be that it has been difficult to pass these values along to our children. "If they could only know what I know, then everything would be fine." Why is that? Because advertising speaks so much louder than we can. So, we remain quiet or say as little as necessary. It's hard to be sure of what's right to say or, worse, to discover that it's difficult to know exactly what we believe. Besides, this is a new generation and things seem to be much better for us than it was for our parents. "This must be the way people of our new socio-economic condition must have lived for generations. Maybe it would be best if we just left well enough alone" . . . and so we do.

There are people who would rather keep quiet but, like hundreds of people I met, I would rather give my children as sound a start toward their financial future as possible. It is important for parents to influence their children's values. After all, if we don't pass along our values consciously, we can't help but do so unconsciously.

There just isn't enough money to get the boom boxes, designer jeans, and required items of social status. As parents, it's important for us to teach our children that society's values can be different from traditional values. These values are neither right nor

wrong, since society is ever changing. But, it is important that each player be aware that these differing
values can put child and parent in conflict.

Children base their values on what they see and
what they hear. If we say, "Always tell the truth," and
they hear us lie to our spouse, our children make a
value judgment. In some cases they may totally reject
what they hear and see as not a real, worthwhile value.
Nonetheless that will be a value-forming observation
— in which case it could have cynical results. They
learn their values from what they see and hear. When
we say violence is not the way and yet allow our
children to witness 18,000 homicides on television by
the time they are eighteen, it's pretty unrealistic to
expect them to embrace the concept of brotherhood,
trust, and kindness by our insistence that violence is
all wrong.

Values are developed every moment of every day.
Have you ever made a conscious effort to define how
you formed your values (or attitudes) as compared to
what your children are basing their values on? That
can be insightful. If you haven't, do give it a try. At the
very least, you will discover that your young person will
listen to what you have to say with absolute interest.
I am certain there is no better way to talk to young
people than to share with them where you're coming
from while acknowledging where they're at. There is
a very real difference between today's societal values

and the baggage (good or not) you brought with you on your journey to this point in time. This baggage has a great influence on how you see and react to the world around you.

Having said all that about values, the purpose is to encourage adults to **talk**, communicate, and otherwise hold discourse with their young friends. Say, "I remember when I was your age. My dad couldn't stand my favorite records. He used to say . . . ." The effect this has on those you influence is unbelievable. Why? Because, you acknowledge who they are and let them know where you're coming from, and it gives everyone a chance to accommodate each other's views. In the four years I devoted to this project I never once heard a young person who was not enthusiastic about hearing where the people important to them were coming from. That's significant.

After a recent talk, a very modern-looking lady mentioned how she thought the financial planning system I outlined was of great value because it would improve the quality of her life. I asked, "How will it affect you?" She said, "I will have money to spend without feeling guilty!" Now, where did she get such an idea? Why did she feel guilt spending her money when, from all appearances, she didn't have to. Actually, it isn't at all unusual. Grandparents taught their children (us) their values which did not emphasize money but, rather, hard work (that's how you and I got to where we are today) and waste not, want not. For our modern lady, her lifestyle was in conflict with some of the values she held about spending money. The idea is to develop a strategy to accommodate both what she learned (the ideas she bought into in her youth) and the realities of today's very different economy.

Did you know that our parents didn't have rummage or garage sales? They had hand-me-downs back then. Rummage sales are a product of this generation . . . waste not, want not is alive and well in suburbia.

"For us there is only the trying, and the rest is not our business."

....Joan Baez

CHAPTER THREE

Children May Not Listen:
"By Way Of Example"

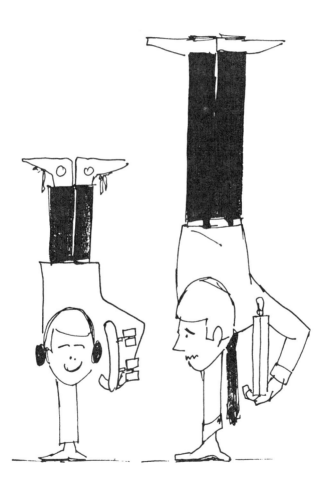

If our past experiences helped shape our parental values for today, what has shaped our children's values? Certainly our parental influence. But today there are additional forces at work which we were not required to contend with in our youth.

It's never been easy teaching young people anything. They require tremendous amounts of energy and produce untold millions for the headache remedy manufacturers. If you have doubts, ask any grandmother.

Yet, in today's economy, the importance of persevering in teaching your child about money at an early age has never been more important. Experts point out that ninety percent of today's homes have one or more television sets, and our children see, on the average, a staggering 20,000 TV commercials each year. Each commercial has only one purpose, to interest and encourage the viewer to buy something.

By the time our youngsters are in their teens, they very likely have access to cash we scarcely dreamed of in our youth. This year, teenagers spent a record $35 billion dollars, and they aren't spending it just on candy and comic books. If you're into statistics, by the time your child has completed the 12th grade, she will have spent 11,000 hours attending school. Compare that to 15,000 hours watching television, which includes six to eight commercials per hour and 17,000 events of human destruction per year . . . on the average.

At $35 billion annually, children become an important part of our economy. Lacking the ability to evaluate the meaning and intent of commercials, they readily put naive trust in advertising claims and then focus their enthusiasm into pressure on parents. We all know how forceful they can be . . . and so do the advertisers. Thirty five billion dollars worth and it's growing at 18% a year!

I still remember working in the hay fields for fifty cents an hour. Hoeing tobacco for seventy five cents an hour was top dollar for a twelve year old, provided you had your own hoe. It just wasn't that easy getting five dollars together. With three dollars in my pocket I was ready to paint the town. What ever happened? I might be over 40, but I was never part of an economy that aimed a billion dollars of advertising at me to target my seventy five cents an hour.

Add to this all the other forms of advertising designed to reach children, and you have, what appears to be, a major assault on our young persons' spending habits and skills with money. It just seems to me that if we parents or grandparents, stepparents, friends, aunts or uncles were ten again, and getting all this marketing aimed at us, we surely would welcome some help. In fifth grade, it just isn't easy being in that trench all alone.

How can children be protected from commercial interests? They can't. How can they be given the skills and ability to deal with the economic realities they face daily? As parents, that's our job. No one else seems to want to do it. Nor should they. More and more schools are beginning to teach basic skills, but the example and ideas young people learn at home are still the most effective lessons. Teaching them about money is more than conveying the values we hold important. It is a tactical maneuver. Why? Because advertisers **don't** say, "Buy our product when you have taken care of your most important needs . . . also, wait until you have compared our claims with the other products on the market . . . and be sure to give consideration to the likelihood that what we advertise may be of no real benefit to you at all."

Home is where our children will learn the most about financial judgments, attitudes toward money, and patterns of money management. No small task! Especially when we realize that, as parents, we are to teach something that more than likely we never had to learn, because we didn't grow up in their kind of world. A bottle of 7-Up and a Baby Ruth candy bar was about it for us. Not so today. Designer jeans,

$70 skate boards, and Walkman stereos that cost more than we made all year are basic to today's advertised standards.

That's why so many in our community are in financial hot water. I remember an incident a couple of years ago when I was visiting one of the apartment buildings we owned. As I examined the shrubs with our maintenance man, I was very much aware of the young couple that had moved in the previous month. Since it was July, they had the windows open. Harsh words disclosed that they were having a first class argument about their finances. It was clear that the husband was upset by his wife's spending practices. She stood accused of carelessly spending money on unnecessary things that should be bought on sale. She, in turn, was irritated by the fact that he wouldn't give her more than a $20 monthly "allowance" to spend as she wanted. Besides, he had his own charge card to buy what he wanted without question . . . even though she recited past due amounts and quoted the demand for full payment within ten days. Money was the trigger, no doubt, that caused this unfortunate confrontation. The exchange continued until the young man said, "You can't have any more because you can't take care of it!" She simply replied, "I've never had any to learn how."

She was 19 and he was 21. Her last comment struck me as profound. That's all too often the case . . . "I've never had any to learn how."

Ten years ago, when these two people were all alone in the trenches, would some help have prevented this dangerous argument? Dangerous because, today, financial disputes are the number one cause of divorce in this country.

By now I hope that I have made my case for spending the necessary time and energy to provide your young person with the assistance to learn how to deal with money in an effective and positive way. From here I will lay out a strategy for effectively teaching your child the value of money. Then, we'll have a cup of coffee and discuss each part in greater detail. I will include some objectives, options, and limitations to each step in this program.

As I said earlier, it's not important that you buy into everything I say, just consider these ideas and choose the ones that fit your unique situation.

Finally, after a little more coffee, we will talk about some ideas that I found very interesting while doing the research for this book — things like kids and credit cards, checkbooks, paying for good grades, and living at home past the school years.

The strategy used in teaching children about money includes the effective use of an allowance, the necessary use of family duties not for pay, and the availability of extra jobs for pay at home.

The upside to this program will be the realization of a higher degree of self-esteem and confidence in your child's life. There will be less bickering over money and these learned skills will be remembered for an entire lifetime.

Of course the downside should also be recognized. It is seen all too often. It's seen on the faces of "not so young" people — a look that shouldn't be on anyone's face in this wonderful, opportunity-filled country. It's the look that comes when we, as parents, realize that the reasons we give ourselves for not taking the time to talk about money matters are the very reasons our children won't develop the skills. Be their example.

> "The hand of the parent writes on the heart of the child the first faint characters which time deepens into strength . . . ."
>
> ....R. Hill

CHAPTER FOUR

Don't Eat The Money:
"Talking And Showing"

Most experts agree that children are able to understand the basics of money at the age of three or four. At this age children are great observers and imitators. For that reason, your example as a role model becomes very important. I found that between three and six, my own children looked up to me and actually believed I was the one person who could make no mistakes. In addition, I could leap tall buildings, do major and minor miracles, and had the power to make anything possible, just by saying so. If I said I would do something and never got around to it, that proved to be very confusing. Why would I promise to do something (after all I could do anything) and then not deliver? That's what being an example is really all about — doing what you say you will.

Talking with children at this age is very important. Evenings seem to work best for most families. The world slows down and the bond of communication is easier to establish. These are important times to explain why you do things the way you do. More importantly, this is the time to encourage children to ask questions. These moments are the times from which memories come.

Sometimes, parents believe they don't know enough about matters like personal finance to explain it to their youngsters. That is seldom the case. It is probably true that most parents have not studied economics and fewer still are versed in the area of investments. But every parent has a great deal of first-hand experience.

Successful parents recall that when their children were four or five they would take them to the grocery store. They talked about what they were looking for, how much it cost, and what considerations they gave to their buying decision. They also laid the ground rules before entering the store. "You may pick out one thing to buy for under fifty cents." Or, "Today I would like you to pick out the big box of Corn Flakes." Or, "I don't have any extra money today, so we won't be able to buy anything that is not on our list."

The importance of all this is that we are willing to talk to our children at an early age about what we have learned. Take the time to honestly answer their questions — even if your answer is, "I really don't know" or "Good question, son, what do you think?"

You've learned from your mistakes, and you've gained confidence from your successes. That's all the background necessary. If an honest answer is, "I don't know," that's OK. Your honesty and sincerity come through and, since you can leap tall buildings, the honesty and sincerity only prove that you care.

After the grocery store, take your daughter with you when you do your banking. She will understand that it's an important place just because she is with you. And there isn't any banker alive who won't give a child a treat. To this day, my two children know which financial institutions give the best goodies and which ones can't be depended upon to see them waving from the back seat of the car.

On the way home talk about the importance of putting money in a safe place, like a credit union or bank, and how you will have your money when you need it. Also talk about where the money that you put in the bank comes from. Explain that one of the very important reasons you go off to work every day is to earn money. Describe in great detail the work you do to earn your money. Follow that up with how she benefits from your work. Name some of the things she has because of it.

I call these trips with mom and dad Visual Tours. At this early age, all of life is a visual tour. Best of all, anyone can provide them. It gives your child the chance to experience places that she most likely will not know about otherwise. When my son, Rolf, was five we did a visual tour of the fire station. We talked about what the fireman's job was and why it's important to all of us. Rolf sat on the fire truck, which was a bright green color. I told him that when I was young all the fire trucks were red, but things change. We talked with real firemen and he discovered that firemen have families, just like us, and when they aren't working they go home to their families, just like when I come home. After that we had an ice cream cone and headed home. Just three hours and together we made a memory.

That evening take the time to recount the events of your special visual tour. Assure your child of your love and that you will always do what's best . . . now go to sleep, Little Fireman.

At this age, our children's learning curve is very high but their attention span isn't. It may seem that they are retaining very little. But, in fact, they are remembering very much. They remember the look on our faces and the tones we use in speaking. They remember the emotion of our stories, if not our message. That is why retelling is important.

As time goes along, they retain more and more of our stories, even to the point of retelling them using our same expression and inflections.

Show your son actual money — a penny, nickel, dime, and quarter. Point out what they look and feel like. Encourage him to identify each coin. Make a game out of showing him how many pennies make a nickel and how many nickels it takes to make a dime. Use real coins and let him ask the questions. Make it an experience and have fun. But, don't eat the money!

Recently, a group of young children was asked to draw various coins. Children who had access to coins only on an occasional basis drew all coins larger than the ones drawn by children who had touched and felt coins frequently. Children with exposure to coins of all denominations had realistic dimensions to relative size. It might be interesting to have your young child do the same and see if coins appear in correct relative size . . . a dime being smaller then a nickel and the quarter being the largest.

Young children think differently than adults in two major areas. First, they have less experience. That is obvious to us but not to them. Secondly, children under nine tend to think in concrete terms. They see that two nickels make a dime, but the nickel is larger and must then be more valuable anyway. Show a five year old a dime and a nickel. Ask him which he would rather have. He'll take the nickel every time. Because of this concrete type of thinking, youngsters can't follow abstract ideas. Talk of saving money for college or the virtue of saving pennies which make dollars for tomorrow just won't get you anything but upset. Limit yourself to challenging the basics but not demanding an in-depth understanding.

Some children of six are going on twelve psychologically and will grasp financial concepts quickly. However, most will require frequent repetition, so limit yourself to what money is (coins and paper bills) and what it does. Patience, boundless patience.

The object of money becomes obvious with each television commercial they see. Take the opportunity to talk to your child about commercials. "Why do they have a commercial in the middle of a good show?" Answer: To encourage you to buy what they have to sell. "Why?" Because the actors and actresses on the show work there to make money just like us. That's how they make their living. They have families and houses to go home to just like the fireman and banker. When people buy the products that are advertised in the commercials, part of the money goes to the actors and actresses who work on the show so they can buy nice clothes and food for their own families.

Remember the television series, "Dukes of Hazzard"? When Rolf and I talked about their commercials, it was a wide eye opener for him to realize that the Duke boys didn't live on the show, but had homes in California just like real people. They bought groceries and went out for dinner with some of the money they earned working on the program.

Preschool, ages three to five, is the time to explore what money is all about — counting, touching, recognizing coins, and learning how to convert a coin into a purchase (Show and Tell). It's like the visual tour to the fire station, financial institution, or police station. It leaves a lasting **positive** impression on young people. They meet real firemen and discover they are people who are there to help in special times of need. It's healthy for them to learn that they are people with families just like us. It is also healthy for them to understand that a commercial is a pitch to get them to want to buy a product that they may or may not need. They must decide if the product is something they need and can afford. Including a trip to your credit union or bank will have the same effect and add to the realization that money is vital to society within the limits of your values.

Why the emphasis on a visual tour of your financial institution? Money matters cause stress. Research shows that most adults have the same reaction to visiting a bank as that of visiting a lawyer or doctor. This feeling can be subconsciously conveyed to your young person. In a society so dependent on money (for better or for worse), it becomes very important not to be intimidated when walking into such a facility. By taking your young person on a visual tour, you relax, and that's good. You're only there for the visual tour. That helps. Besides, let your credit union or bank do what it does best . . . public relations.

Any teller or loan officer will always be happy to take a couple of minutes to talk to a youngster, and include a piece of gum or a balloon to make friends fast. While talking to these people it's always good to point out that all these people are working and have families and a home where they go at night, just like we do.

Young people are very much a part of their public relations program. If it weren't for us and our children, they couldn't open their doors on Monday.

Will they really take your child seriously? You bet! Just like the fire station which is tax supported (and every firefighter knows that), every credit union and bank knows that by making people comfortable they will have a loyal, future customer when they buy their first car. After all, they are in the money renting business. Just like sitting on the seat of the fire truck, it's the small things added together that make the difference.

Our honesty and communication at that early age is what our children will remember and respond to. It doesn't matter if we're fully informed on the subject. There will be plenty of time for them to back us into the corner in about ten years. And, who knows, by that time, if we talk to them enough and go on lots of special visual tours, they might not do that to us. That's how it works. For preschoolers it's honesty, conversation, and visual tours.

When Rolf was five, he really wanted to go out and fly a kite. I remembered the fun I had at that age with the kite my dad had made with me. Also, it seemed like a good way to show Rolf the advantages of saving money (knowing about concrete thinking I still thought I had a good idea). Since he saved (reluctantly) three of the dollars he received for his birthday, I planned to reinforce the advantages of saving. He now could have something that he really wanted and had saved for for a long time . . . most of two weeks. Having not spent his money on things like candy (free at the bank) he could now have his kite.

So off we went to the store to get a kite for a buck and a half. $8.79!! Good grief! What ever happened to kite prices? Incredible . . . unbelievable.

After I recovered from my foray into the preschooler's world of commercial reality, I quickly concluded that we both live in the same world. It's no cheaper for Rolf than for good old dad. I was caught in my lesson and paid the additional money for Rolf's kite. We left, with me still determined to provide him with a valuable lesson. Creativity and communication had to be the key.

When we arrived home, Rolf quickly set about showing everyone his colorful kite. There was my opportunity. While we opened everything up, and Rolf was listening, I voiced my surprise to Sandy (the other half of this marriage) at the cost of today's kites. I talked about how prices have gone up and what I used to pay for a really first-class kite. Also, I described how I had intended to show Rolf how he could save small amounts of money to buy something big that he really wanted. And that hadn't quite worked out the way I had intended. Did this conversation serve any good purpose?

Today Rolf is eleven, and we have laughed as **he** has retold the story of the day we went to town to buy his first kite. He tells it from the perspective of my conversation with Sandy, including my plan to teach him all about saving. He doesn't miss the part about my surprise at the store when I found out how prices had gone up. Imagine Dad not knowing how much a kite costs! And the entire story will be around for Rolf's children to hear.

It's just one example of how a lesson, even one that didn't go as planned, can have a lasting impact, with positive results.

Preschoolers learn so much by observation. They learn by example and they learn fast. Your child probably goes with you shopping, to the bank, and other places where financial transactions take place. Here are some ideas that will provide lasting talks and lessons. When you're in the grocery store, ask your child to help. The task can be getting the two biggest apples from the produce table or a small box of Corn Flakes. If your five year old is going on 16, ask her, "Which of these two do you think is the best buy, three small cans or the one large can?"

Because of limits on your time, there will be occasions when these conversations will not be possible. But, do give them choices as often as possible. A planned trip is best, and you'll feel great after it's finished. And when there is no time, say so. Don't let it make you feel guilty.

The next time you take your child banking with you, ask these questions, "Do you know what I am doing at this credit union?" "What will these people do with the money I give them?" "What do you think the person behind that desk does for us?" "Do you know why they always give you a piece of candy or a balloon?" Take time for your child to meet someone at your bank and, if possible, spend a few minutes letting your child talk with that person.

Whenever we take Kari and Rolf on any visual tour, we always explain the financial ground rules first. "You may go on four rides" — even an amusement park can be a visual tour. Setting the ground rules does two things. First, we are not embarrassed by our children begging for things off the grocery shelf in an otherwise stone-quiet store. Secondly, they get their first experience in using money. At a flea market, we let them buy any one item that costs less than a dollar, or perhaps two. It doesn't teach them all they need to know but it gives them a place to begin.

One couple related how they had explained the ground rules of spending no more than two dollars at a garage sale. Their daughter soon returned with purchases well in excess of her dollar limit. Questioning revealed that she had used her big blue eyes and the plea that she had only two dollars and besides, "I'm so little." Kids learn by observation and they learn fast.

CHAPTER FIVE

The Three Part Allowance

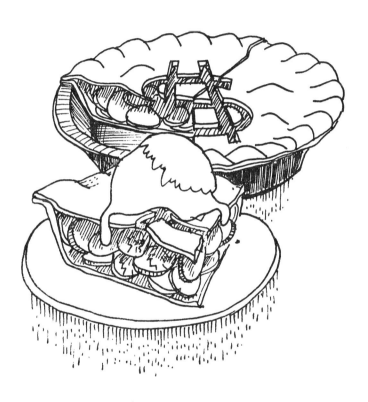

In the previous chapter we covered three very important foundation elements for teaching children about money. At first glance they may appear to have nothing at all to do with our objective. Be assured they are very important and should be used as the children grow well into their teen years. These three tools are the visual tours, show and tell, and short talks. Visual tours are important because preschool children learn by observation. Show and tell is significant because much of learning about money is the act of seeing, comparing, and handling money under supervision. Finally, we should recognize the absolute value of our communications. Talking about commercials gives our children a perspective on what is being aimed at them and why. Because of their open, naive view of television, they need to understand the purpose of commercial messages.

In this chapter we will begin discussing another three elements necessary to develop an understanding of personal finance. Most young people are quick and eager to learn, but they tend to get bored quickly. But then, along with concrete thinking, what else is new? The real reward is watching their personalities develop and blossom.

Of all the tools available to teach young people about money management, none is better than the allowance. An allowance by itself, however, does not contain the complete solution. Let me explain.

Think of the allowance as a three-part program. The Allowance is a set amount of money given, more or less unconditionally, at fixed time periods. The second and third elements of the program are Family Responsibilities and Extra Income Opportunities.

The allowance is an amount of money given at a fixed time each week. It should be given unconditionally because of who your child is . . . a member of your family who is unique and special. An allowance should not be money the young person must spend as the parent dictates.

The amount of the allowance is dependent upon your financial situation. A national survey recently showed that children at age five received $1.40 on the average per week with a more or less consistent increase to $8.25 at age 16. These are averages with a couple of interesting points. First, boys get more than girls of the same age. Can you believe it? This unfortunate situation is corrected in the teen years because, I suspect, girls pay for a greater portion of their personal needs than boys do.

Secondly, as the economic level of parents increase, the amount of allowance is lower. There appears to be a need for more affluent parents to teach their children the value of working for what they get from life, while parents in lower economic situations want their children to enjoy a better life than what they had worked for.

Overall, the average allowance is $3.30 per week. That figure in itself really has no meaning. When setting the allowance, the amount should be based on your economic situation and what your child will be spending the money on. If, for example, your daughter is to pay for school lunches out of her allowance, then the amount will likely have to be larger than $3.

When deciding the amount of the allowance, it must be enough for your child to buy something. If not, he will lose interest. This is not the time to be teaching savings. I maintain that the amount of the allowance must be like priming a well. It shouldn't quench the thirst, but it must be enough to make it work. At six, Rolf could recognize and count coins. He received fifty cents a week. That was great as a starter in the rural midwest where we choose to live, but a child in New York City would require substantially more.

It is very important that there is enough money for your child to spend freely as he or she wants.

Under the age of twelve, it is my recommendation that an allowance not be tied to any other financial responsibility. Therefore, the amount would be lower than with other considerations included, like school lunches or clothing. The problem with including other spending requirements in an allowance is that we are trying to teach kids to manage money. The amount they manage must be large enough to spend, but not so large they aren't required to make any decisions. What would you do if your eight year old came home from school and said he didn't have any money for lunch tomorrow because he just doesn't have any money left. Where did it go? "I don't know" is the certain reply. Why put yourself through it? Lunch is important and I have observed that any important, health-affecting responsibility should not be placed on a not yet responsible person. Your child will have the opportunity to learn responsibility with the second part of this program.

Once the amount has been agreed upon, agree on where the allowance will be given — "At home, on Saturday, after lunch."

In our previous life, Rolf would hit me up for his allowance anytime we were within 75 meters of a video game. What do you do? Make it clear where and when the pay-off is to be made. Don't wait to be caught in the stone-quiet store where there is no escape for an unprepared parent. Rolf never misses his Saturday pay-off at the kitchen table, and I am never caught unsure if he is, in fact, due for his allowance.

It may seem unnecessary to talk to your children about the amount of the allowance they are to receive. At first the tendency is to give too little. Why? Because, if all they do is spend it on candy and video games, it just doesn't make sense to provide more than a dollar. Maybe so, but the price you paid for your first kite wasn't what it is today either. Of greater importance, talk to them about how they intend to spend their allowance. Maybe you can't have a real heavy dialogue with a five year old, but as your children get older they begin to understand that the allowance is to them what your paycheck is to you. The allowance is a child's first introduction to a consistent, reliable form of income. A good question to ask is, "What do you intend to do with your allowance?" Next year the answer will be different. Kari spends a full fifty percent of her allowance at the bookstore (and the other half paying her fines at the library).

Kids come in all forms. The twelve year old that's emotionally going on six will not warrant as large an allowance as the eight year old who is a math whiz and needs the cash to buy replacement computer disks. How can you know? Talk to them and listen to what they say.

To be effective, an allowance should be given unconditionally and it shouldn't be money that they have to spend on things we, the parents, tell them. Without that freedom, the ability to make their own spending decisions can't happen. Later, in the early teen years, non-discretionary spending can be introduced. At six through ten, however, money is to learn with and children should be free to spend it, save it, or blow it away foolishly. We might not approve of our children's spending, in fact it is doubtful we will ever approve of their spending, but they will learn more from seeing a cheap toy broken on the way home than from a lecture by us on the virtues of thrift for rainy days. This is the single best reason to keep the amount of the allowance within reason.

Any parent who provides an allowance of twenty dollars a week for an eight year old is building some pretty unrealistic expectations for that child in about five or six years. And that parent will be dealing with those expectations on an entirely different level at that time. No thanks.

For the same reason, it is important to explain to our children that their allowance is their portion of the family's income, a portion they are entitled to just because they are members of this family. To help build self-esteem and family pride, the allowance should be regarded as their share of the family's financial fortunes and not something that has to be deserved or wheedled from their parents.

Should the parent ever intervene in the child's spending? Well, the idea is to become skilled in guiding the child, through hints and suggestions, without nagging. Talking with each other during the quiet times will help your child develop an understanding of the reasons involved in spending decisions. Talking will enable your child to understand your family's understood standards (values). You do have an obligation to step in if your son is saving to buy a machine gun or porno video, but purchases that are merely foolish should never be vetoed. Let him make his own mistakes now, while the stakes are small. Without your positive support, suggestions, and guidance, there is no other way to learn which things are of real value. Sometimes it seems like you're just trying to hold onto a greasy rope over a den of snakes. You have no other choice but to hang on and do your best. I have discovered that doing anything positive with children will turn out OK. They have a resilience that will always carry them through every fear every parent has.

Try not to intervene when your daughter spends her couple of dollars on the dumbest thing money can buy. I know that is no small task. I've been there a thousand times and so has every other adult who has their children's best interests at heart. It's not easy, but it is important to let them make their own decisions and for us to point them in the best direction we know, the best way we know.

The second part of an effective allowance program is each child's responsibilities to the family unit. Everything in life operates on the principle of cause and effect. It's the same in every family. It is important for children to learn that with an unconditional allowance, they have to assume responsibilities within their family. These are obligations we depend on one another to fulfill for the good of the entire family. For better or for worse, every family member is in this together. That's important to realize.

Duties are different in each family. If both parents work, the duties of each family member reflects that circumstance. If a family member has special needs, the responsibilities of the rest must reflect those needs. The bottom line is, every member of every family must participate in helping that family progress according to each other's capabilities, just as they share in the family's fortunes (allowance).

At age six, these family responsibilities can include setting and clearing the table, taking care of their room, feeding the family pet, and/or taking the trash out. With Rolf and Kari, we discussed their new allowances and how they planned to use them. Then, because we rely on one another in our family, they each were given three tasks. Rolf became responsible for his room, the downstairs bathroom, and emptying all waste baskets. Kari became responsible for her room, the upstairs bathroom, and dusting all downstairs rooms.

The idea is to have children recognize these responsibilities as doing their part in the family without needing constant reminders to carry out their duties.

It does take encouragement and patience . . . endless patience. By the time Rolf was ten, he became the king of clean bathrooms. No one can do a better job. He still needs an occasional reminder every other week, but he gets it done without any complaints and does it right. Encouragement and endless patience do have their rewards. Not perfection by any means, but the small steps of progress are measurable.

Encouragement is given in terms of our reliance upon our children to do their part. After all, if we can't count on each other, who can we really count on? I think the concept of cooperation is an idea that most young children can understand. Plan to invest a lot of time when your young person is five, six, and seven talking about how we depend on one another. Sharing our monetary resources goes hand in hand with recognizing our responsibilities to each other. Is that an easy task to face? Not on your life, but I can't imagine it any other way. Communication and patience, endless patience.

As allowances increase, so do the family responsibilities. Today, Rolf continues to empty waste baskets and do his other tasks. Also, he takes our four trash cans out to the road for the Monday morning pickup. This past winter was not easy for him. Imagine trying to return four empty trash cans to the garage on a plastic sled in a December wind. Our driveway is 800 feet long. That requires encouragement and firmness.

Learning responsibility is not easy, but it starts young and is learned by degrees. And a cup of hot chocolate when he comes in is a reward for a job well done.

Kari is a first class cook. In addition to her previous responsibilities she now has kitchen duty with her brother. Could the kitchen be neater? You bet. And we could do without some of the bickering that goes on between them in the kitchen. I figure it's only to get our attention, and they are in the process of learning to work things out without our parental intervention. Kari's family responsibilities now include the care and feeding of our animals which number three horses, two dogs, one llama, and a bunch of barn cats. Her duties are real. That is, we depend on her. Without Kari's and Rolf's help, things would have to change for us.

We have made a point to provide responsibilities that are **not** "make work" or that are solely for our comfort. I encourage you to give special consideration to your young person's family responsibilities. Their greatest purpose must be to foster high self-esteem and a feeling of certainty in belonging to the family unit. Without that, we're all alone.

With an allowance and family responsibilities in hand, what about earning money for special events like birthdays and holidays? Vacations usually require amounts of money that only older children have the ability to plan for. Younger children, below the age of ten, tend to live week to week, allowance to allowance, without any thought of putting a portion of their income away for that special trip. Of course, most allowances are not structured to provide an incentive to save for special events. Nevertheless, these times do arrive and parents are left in a position of saying, "Now what do I do?"

If we reach into our pockets regularly, as most special events tend to be spaced thoughout the year, the benefit of the allowance can be lost. Soon, we begin to realize that the allowance experience is no more than a money supply to augment special events. That's not good! Neither child nor parent will recognize any lasting gain from this practice.

Many parents I interviewed have developed a very successful method of providing extra income opportunities to enable their children to add to their allowance money. The implementation and actual practice vary with individual situations including income, family size, age of the children, geographic location, rent or own, and whether the family resides in a metropolitan or rural setting. The psychological age and physical ability of each youngster certainly is a considered factor as well.

Extra income opportunities are simply the first real job a youngster ever has. It is the third aspect of the allowance program and should be part of the allowance from the very beginning. In each of the cases I viewed, the basic implementation was the same even though the actual practice varied within the limits I previously mentioned.

Wherever we live, there are things that we might consider paying someone to do for us. Washing windows, washing and waxing the family car, sweeping the garage, all sorts of work around the lawn, painting (a definite age consideration), weeding the garden, shining shoes, cleaning the refrigerator, organizing the lawn shed, and cleaning the barn are all possibilities to be considered as jobs to increase income. The vague distinction between family responsibilities and extra income opportunities is that extra income opportunities will tend to be more or less one time tasks and not repeated each week like family responsibilities. A job like washing the windows, done once or twice a year, makes a great extra income opportunity. But cleaning a bathroom is a weekly responsibility. What about watching baby sister or mowing the lawn? Most families use these types of jobs as major income opportunities above and beyond normal family responsibilities.

Yes, it could get a little complicated. Should the lawn mowing be a family responsibility or is it for extra income? How about meal preparation when both parents work? And what about kitchen patrol and washing evening dishes? When that is happening, listen to what everyone has to say and then pick a number, any number . . . and remember you are the extra income opportunity. End of that story!

Extra income opportunities are a great way to prepare young people to be self sufficient. As they get older, they realize that they have more control over their financial situation. This sense of self confidence begins to show in all areas of their lives.

Sandy and I have a list of things that we would prefer not to do. Rolf and Kari are eager workers . . . well, not always, but reminding them of events or activities they should be planning for will bring out the list. After all, their allowances provide them with only a small portion of what they feel they need (that would also be true if their allowances were double what they are today). That's what I mean by priming the well.

When a job is done, Sandy or I look it over and level honest criticism, if it's warranted (tactfully as possible), or honest praise when it's earned. We criticize because it is their first job and because this way they can learn about the standards that future employers expect. If the job performance is lacking they can correct the deficiency or earn less for the work.

What's a job worth? That depends on you. It must be a service that you can use. In other words it must be real and not busy work. Kids will see through that in a second and their performance will reflect that attitude.

Start with a list of ten or more things you would be willing to compensate your young person for. Then assign a dollar (or cents) value to each listed job. Consider the age, ability, and motivation of your young person. When you discuss the allowance, present the extra income opportunities in a positive and supportive light.

Two years ago, Kari agreed to clean the chicken house for $5. Not only had she not surveyed the scope of the task, but, when she did, she asked us to reconsider the price. Her point was that the job would take six or seven hours and that $7 was a fairer price. If we agreed, she would also be willing to rake the chicken yard. She did the job and earned a real "well done" compliment besides.

I don't care for cleaning the chicken house, and it was Kari's suggestion that $7 was a fair price. Her gain was also the realization that she has the ability to earn the money for whatever she perceives her needs to be. There is no doubt in my mind that had I simply given her $7 she would have valued it far less than having worked to earn it.

When you select extra income opportunity work, recognize that perfection will not be apparent with your children any more than if you hired someone outside your family to do the same work. We try to be flexible. To be honest, we consider the purpose for which Rolf and Kari are earning the money. If they want to pursue something that we encourage, we will accept a lower degree of perfection than if they plan to make a purchase we are less enthusiastic about. We are flexible because they are our children. As parents we can do that. Also, there is less parental guilt if we stay flexible.

Also, I have noticed that my performance expectations increase the closer I get to the house. That must be because I don't have to live in the barn. If a job must be repeated, children soon learn — "not good." And they do better next time.

Metropolitan and country kids have real income opportunities. They may be very different, however, neither location is lacking in opportunity for the youngster with a parent who has developed a resourceful eye.

It is important to remember that jobs are service oriented and that our children might be asked to do the same task for a neighbor. The good news is that they will generally do a better job for the neighbor. According to a certain grandmother, that was true when I was nine.

An interesting point. Young people under the age of twelve do not like working by the hour. They prefer to be paid by the job. If your daughter is a reluctant participant, her inability to relate the job to the time it takes to do it may be the cause. On the other hand, she can quickly understand that a job is worth a $1.25 exchange for her time.

Young people also expect their job performance to be evaluated. This seems to be a carry over from school and makes sense. As a parent, be assured that job performance will increase 50% when your young person works for the neighbor. I think that's a cultural thing that we perpetuated when we were young and therefore have no control over. It sounds good, anyway. In ten or twelve years when your young charges are on their own and doing so well, you can sit back and say, "I had something to do with that, you know!"

"Can anyone remember when times were not hard and money scarce?"
....Ralph Waldo Emerson

CHAPTER SIX

Influences: "It's Not Just Talking"

The Allowance, Family Responsibilities, and Extra Income Opportunities, when used together, add up to building a firm foundation for understanding the value of money at a time when the price for making mistakes is least expensive. For a parent, this can be the hardest part.

With money in our children's pockets, how can we influence their spending and form habits that will last a lifetime?

What they choose to spend money on is influenced by several forces. First is the advertising they receive from television and their favorite magazines. When kids view ads they learn one thing, how to spend money. Secondly, teenagers are influenced by their peer group. As parents, we must recognize the strong force peer pressure exerts and the need for acceptance by their peer group.

Without exception, the experts and the people I talked with all over this country agree that to effectively influence and build good spending habits there must be interested communication between parent and child. I use the term interested because it seems that communication is not enough. As parents, we must be interested in what interests and concerns our children. Just talking to or with them is not necessarily communicating with them. I am the first to say that what an eight year old is interested in is not necessarily what I am going to be interested in. I have, however, found that admitting that to an eight year old will have a positive effect.

That being the case, I was told how a father took his daughter to a restaurant for dinner. What an occasion that was for her. They had the greatest conversation while the young lady felt very special to have her dad all to herself. The two way communication was terrific as they talked about peer pressure and dad's concerns and hopes for his daughter.

On another occasion, the other parent took her son to a movie, followed with a pizza and all the conversation they could have. In addition to the social skills these two young people learned, consider the positive influence it had upon relieving peer pressure. What an idea!

Kari, Rolf and I have the best conversations while driving in the car (though never with both together) or during a late-night session in their rooms. The value of these situations is obvious, but how often do we **not** act upon them when they are presented to us?

When Rolf was eight and had a dollar in his pocket, his sole mission in life was to divest himself of carrying it any longer then thirty minutes. The vision of money

burning a hole in his pocket must have been a terrify-
ing thought because it is clear he was determined to
get that dollar back into circulation. No amount of
talking, hints, or insistence helped. Forget suggestions.
At the very least he was determined to spend his
allowance to buy something to give away. To whom?
Who knows! The job was to spend the allowance.
Never mind the details, just get out of his way, he had
his job to do.

It is only my opinion, but I feel this condition is
directly proportional to the amount of TV a young
person watches. My opinion was reinforced by the
revelation that greater progress was visibly made after
TV viewing was limited to his performance . . . as
disclosed by his report card.

At this age (under ten) Kari also enjoyed spending
her allowance in the fast lane at the Ben Franklin store
just as much as Rolf. Kari, who didn't have Rolf's
allergies to corn products, could be much more
graceful at the checkout counter. Rolf's choices were
cut in half, and, to his credit, he seldom slipped and
bought any corn-based product.

It was after the kite project that I knew something
had to yield. As it turned out, it was me. TV is a per-
manent part of our society. To its credit it provides
programs that take you inside the human heart, across
the Himalayas, into space, and under the ocean. It gets
my vote. However, we have to recognize the power its

commercial messages have on us and our children.

How do you compete with today's commercial bombardment? Every fifteen minutes they teach buy, buy, buy! For Sandy and me, Kari was easy. She enjoys reading and realized her allowance could be used to buy books. No problem, I approve. She also loves horses and would save and work the extra income opportunities to the limit for riding lessons. Great! You get the picture.

Well, picture this. Rolf goes from six to seven and then eight years old. His allowance goes from fifty cents to a dollar a week. Then two dollars a week. Rolf would work at any job he was given with all his heart, with or without extra pay. He did the best he could and not once . . . well, seldom . . . would he complain.

Then, I would take him to the mall so he could exercise his spending skills. We would talk about what he wanted to buy and where he might find just what he was looking for. When we arrived at the mall, he would get out of the car, take a deep breath and PUFF! his pockets would burst into flames. Spending goals and all that talk went right out the ventilating system.

Generous? You bet! He would give you his last dollar, both rocks and anything else he might have in his pockets. But, once he got into the trenches it was hopeless. What's a parent to do? Spending, even with abandon, is sometimes necessary but will drive any deserving parent to checking out Clairol color charts.

Then, late one summer the Star Wars movie came to town. Rolf was captivated by that film. He dedicated himself to becoming a Jedi knight. He focused on the Star Wars story and was determined to have every action figure known to man. At last he had a Hot Button! That's the clue that your youngster is ready to learn about the concept of saving and other important financial virtues.

Hot buttons are very interesting. They turn adults on, too. Sometimes it's a car. Some people live hunting and fishing. That's their hot button. You can have a friend for life if you just find his hot button and share his interest.

When I first became an airline pilot, I would go on three and four-day flights. Being new, it was normal to be nervous and concerned about doing the best possible job for the captain who sat three feet to my left. A four-day trip could be an eternity had it not been for the sensitivity most of these men displayed. They were well aware of my newness and nervousness. So, whenever possible they would inquire about my interests, hobbies, or past flying experiences. By doing this they would find something we both had in common which we could focus on. This would enable me to relax and do a better job as their first officer.

It wasn't long before I learned to use the same technique on the salty old captains who were as pleased to have a new pilot with them as having a tooth pulled. Working with someone for four days, with less than three feet between us, had the potential for being a very long time. By looking for their hot button, I could locate an area of interest that we both could focus on for an enjoyable four-day trip.

Rolf's first hot button was the Star Wars saga. He read about it, **saved** his money to join the official fan club, and decided to become a Jedi. What an opening! We talked about how Jedis have to save money for college, and the next day he put on his Jedi robe and opened his first savings account.

That's how we must let our children make their own decisions. It's guided, but it's effective and brings the parent and the child to a mutual point of focus. It takes time and patience, infinite patience. Is it worth it? For parents to remain a competitive force with their child's peer group it is a must. We have no other choice. First, children must learn the **fun** of money, then they learn what it can do for them. Who cares about a home in the country at age nine? Being a Jedi knight is where it's at . . . that's the future! Once they have a vision of what goal setting does for their lives, it's only a short time before they realize that a passbook has as much kick as a Jedi's light saber.

I am of the opinion that if we, as adults, spent a little more time in our kids world of imagination, we would be a lot healthier . . . and closer to our children.

Consider how the advertising world creates an ad that simply starts where a young person's mind is. They don't require a ten year old to change his expectations at all. There they are, running their GI Joe action figures around the lawn and into the vacant lot. That gets right to the imaginary level of the ten year old. Why don't parents do the same? All it takes is time and interest. I am the first, however, to admit that I could never remain there for over an hour . . . certainly never a full afternoon. I think that's OK. I can tell Rolf that fifteen minutes is all I can take of his ten-year-old world. At forty, it's necessary for me to make that clear.

When we enter their world, we can affect their way of looking at things faster than if we insist they play only by our rules.

We live in a NOW society. We adults know it. Every commercial message, every ad says NOW. If we parents realize it and still are influenced by their message, how can we expect our children to catch on by themselves? With a little conversation from mom and dad, they will.

That's where those golden moments become very important. For Sandy and me, living in the country has helped. To get anywhere, to do anything beyond our home, usually requires driving. This has developed into one of the best times to talk to our kids about commercial appeals — money, goal setting . . . even sex. The latter, however, got me a $44.50 traffic citation for going through a stop sign. I suggested to Sandy that sex be banned in automobiles. She, of course, pointed out the futility of my idea.

Find your best place and make time to talk. Bedtime, driving, or the dinner table provide an excellent opportunity to reinforce those ideas that peer groups and advertising slogans constantly challenge. Be as casual as possible (as opposed to authoritarian) and try to listen to your kids as you would if the neighbor kids wanted to have a conversation with you.

Short talks such as these require patience (infinite patience) and repetition. The most rewarding conversation we can have is when our children understand that their allowance is unconditional. It is not associated with a behavior code (other than a life-threatening activity), but it is given to them because they are a member of our family which carries certain responsibilities with its membership. Using money as a reward or punishment can build in a child an association between feelings (advertising and peer pressure both build on feelings and emotions) and material "things." It's only a short step from this kind of association to a tendency to put a price tag on morality. And recent research tends to back this up.

Use the allowance, but in association with family responsibilities and extra income opportunities.

CHAPTER SEVEN

Growing, Growing, Growing: "Tough Stuff"

Throughout this book our focus has been on children less than thirteen years old. This is because the financial learning experience has to begin as early as possible. Most certainly it should begin by the time children reach the age of understanding that the TV commercial presents something they can't go on living without. That is why the Short Talk about actors having families and commercials wanting to sell us something is so important. Show and Tell provides a means for the young person to learn the mechanics of money and making change, while the Visual Tour is effective in providing the realization for your child that there are different people doing interesting and different things for their families, **just like you**. It gives them the opportunity to open their eyes to our dependence on each other.

At the same time it is good to introduce the allowance. But first, gather around the table and have a discussion about the amount. You may already know how much they will receive, but take a half hour to listen and hear what they have to say. Be certain to discuss:

1. Why they receive the allowance — because they are part of the family. How much? What do they intend to do with their allowance (insight time)? Where will the allowance be given? A very, very important strategy. Agree when and where the allowance will be paid (e.g., at the kitchen table on Saturday mornings — never in a public place).

2. An allowance is unconditional, if at all possible. (More about "unconditional" in the last chapter.)

3. The amount of the allowance is related to your family's means. Sounds almost biblical.

4. The allowance is not attached to any behavior code, except a life-threatening activity such as buying drugs or guns. You get the idea.

5. Specify if the allowance is to include a specific purchase, e.g., school lunch money, etc. Do try to avoid any of these restrictions.

6. The greater the allowance, the greater the youngster's family responsibilities, according to age and ability.

A list of each youngster's family responsibilities must be accompanied with an explanation of how these responsibilities relate to your child's membership in the family and how it is a large part of the allowance program.

1. Define family responsibilities in terms of importance to the family.
2. Make a list of each child's responsibilities and when they are to be completed.
3. The greater the allowance the greater the responsibilities. (Same as number 6 on page 65.)

Extra income opportunities should be discussed with a couple of example jobs suggested by you, the parent. In all probability you will not get much of a response from a five or six year old but, as extra money is needed, suggesting any of your listed opportunities may capture interest. Here is where teenagers should begin to see the light.

Actually, this entire program can be introduced at any time through the mid-teen years. Of course, the amounts, conditions, and the approach will vary depending on the age of the children when the program is presented. I would suggest that when your teenage daughter has a W2 earnings job (paycheck), she may very well be beyond the advantages presented here. At this point in her life, if your working teenager has had no money management preparation, introducing it would be a real challenge. Should that be the case, she must come to the realization, on her own, that her financial management needs attention. No amount of reminders from the parent will be of any benefit. Or so the experts (grandparents) tell me.

In this chapter I would like to begin talking about three remaining elements of money and value. Like allowances, these should be introduced (ideally) by six or seven but can be presented into the teen years. It's always better late, than never.

These three elements are savings, charity, and compounding.

The first of these, savings, becomes evident with the discovery of a hot button. Point out how, when your son successfully saved the few dollars required for his last hot button purchase, he decided what he wanted and went after it **and** was successful. Focus on his success. Acknowledge any difficulties he may have had (so you're credible). Really focus on what he did right and how he achieved his goal.

Now, with patience and firmness, ask your children about the way they want to live their lives. If they are in their teens their future plans may be more realistic. Nevertheless talk about how they want to live their lives. It may surprise you, but, after their third day at school, young children will have begun making judgments about other people based on their dress, where they live, and how they look. I am not saying that's right nor am I saying they should **not** be accepting others on character and human qualities. All I am pointing out is that TV, ads, peer groups, and mom and dad each add small pieces to the big perception picture and, if you want to be effective, don't deny or pretend it doesn't happen. They still are the great kids they will always be, as long as apples remain apples to both of you.

Take your daughter on a visual tour of a less fortunate area of town and ask her if that's the way she wants to live. Drive slowly and have a good look. She will always say no, never!

This visual tour may seem a little intense. But, to get to the real emotional level needed to say what we feel, it is important to experience it. This trip is the other side of life's coin. Be assured that it will provide an experience that won't soon be forgotten and will provide many reflective hours of real conversation. The fact is, there is a less fortunate world that exists and it's not far from our own home. There are people who are less fortunate, for very real reasons that are of no fault of their own — real lack of opportunity, lack of education, lack of a role model, or any of a dozen frightful things that can happen to our lives that are beyond our control.

Most people, and children in particular, feel a real sense of emotion toward individuals less fortunate than themselves. Our children will not want to live under the conditions they see on the visual tour, nor will they be any less thankful to us for the opportunities they now enjoy. Reminders like that are good for parents on occasion, also.

With the media programming of spend now and enjoy everything, we have come up against a very large task. That's why the visual tour is essential. It's emotional (or should be) and will reach into a young person faster than any lecture from mom and dad. At this point, real life will serve as a much stronger example than "When I was your age . . . " stories. As important as this subject is and as unreliable as this economy has become, it's necessary to use the most effective teaching tools at hand. Honest emotional impact will outsell a TV commercial two to one, every time. Who knows, maybe the impact will reach parents as well; the United States has one of the lowest savings rates of the entire world.

Isn't using a visual tour to this extent a little radical? No. Peer pressure, TV, and drugs make that trench really hard to live in unless our children have some powerful and honest help. There are other people in this world. This visual tour only shows how some of them have to live and why. The lesson for this visual tour is, "There are situations in life where we can lose control of many things. We must prepare for what we can and be thankful for the rest."

In order to save we all need reasons. The visual tour can provide good reasons. These reasons become goals. Help your son understand and set goals. First, write down what he wants; then, what it will cost, if it has a price tag; and, finally, note when the goal is to be a reality. College is easy to set as a goal. But one guy said to me that his kids are too young to know what they want. You may think so, but they aren't.

Rolf wanted to be a Jedi. I didn't think that was possible, and fortunately I kept it to myself. That goal has led him to a green belt in Karate and a college savings fund for Jedis.

Today, he doesn't want to be a Jedi. But, he has the habit of saving money, and he won't give that up. He doesn't save as much as I would like him to, but it's his idea. He understands why he is doing it. He has replaced his Jedi goal with becoming a physicist, complete with a recitation of Newton's law and a brand new microscope.

How much should a young person save? From those I have talked to, it seems 10% is the hoped for amount. That is dependent upon income and inclination — that is to say, parental encouragement and emotional maturity.

On one of my layovers with the airline, I talked with a retired couple in Las Vegas about what they consciously did to teach their kids the value of money. After talking for thirty minutes, the man turned to his wife and said, "Hard work is how you and I got to where we are today, if only we could convey some appreciation of that to our children now." Let's begin with a visual tour and a heart to heart talk. Heart to heart means, if you as a parent do not save, admit it.

But, don't condone **not** saving. Save together.

You may consider including savings as an issue when talk of an increase in allowance is detected on the jungle drums. Many parents use matching funds. That is, "whatever you put into savings for X goal, we will match with a similar amount." X is usually college or some form of education. Why not take your kids on a visual tour of your local college campus? They will usually have public activities anyone can attend and a student union for coffee and soft drinks after.

Are kids able to draw from their savings account? Yes, if it's money saved by the young person and to be used for the purpose of the savings such as a car or college. It's goal realization time. Celebrate! Seldom is it permitted when matching funds from parents are involved; and never, if the money was saved for college and the young person plans to use it for clothes, etc. The one exception I was able to identify was if the savings were for a specific goal, say college, and the student wanted to join the senior high French class going to France. Flexibility means judgment calls.

Why not several savings accounts? Nothing wrong with one for the car, one for college, one for France, or one for any other important purpose. All good Jedi knights have them.

Encourage pre-teens to make a want list. When Kari was eight she had a "Whim Thing." It was a list of everything she would ever want. Its real intent was to give us a list from which to choose birthday and Christmas gifts that she would enjoy. Soon it turned into her early goal list. If she kept any item on the list for a length of time it wasn't a whim and was considered a gift possibility. Kari would keep it updated with the latest book titles she wanted and delete those she already had.

She is able to use birthday and gift money to get one or two items from her whim list. However, I am impressed with her early practice of crossing off whims that didn't hold up to the test of time for her. This really was her first experience with decision making and that is how money is saved . . . by making the decision that you have enough reasons to do it. According to my banker, fewer than 20 out of every 100 Americans actively save. Rolf and Kari may not save as much as I would like them to, but they have the habit and that puts them in the top 20%. That deserves a celebration . . . tonight it's pizza on me.

Kids see parents with all the money and think adults can do anything they want with it. We need to talk to our kids so they can see that we have to choose what we can and can not buy (after the bills are paid). We, as the parents, must weigh our purchase decisions. The only way our children can ever know that is if we explain it to them. Take the time, it's worth it.

Charity, or giving to the less fortunate, is one more very important part of learning the value of money.

People say to me, "But, I barely have enough for myself. Hey, if I had a million dollars I would be happy to give a hundred thou or so to the poor." I'm not so sure. If people don't learn to share when the amounts are small, they just aren't going to suddenly change their style when the amounts are larger . . . and from charity comes purpose.

My friend Jim Rohn says, "The act of giving should be taught early in life. The best time to teach a child the act of charity is when he gets his first dollar. Take him to a place where people are truly helpless so that he learns compassion. If a child understands, he won't have any trouble parting with a dime. Children have big hearts."

Plan a visual tour and explain that church organizations, service clubs, scouts, and 4-H clubs all work to help the less fortunate. It's another way to give of yourself to help others. Sure, we hear of all the free loaders that lurk just around the corner, but don't focus on them if you want to remain healthy. There are so many who desperately need help. They aren't just in Africa. These people are close to you and me. They need our help. By helping them, our children become more responsible, mature, purposeful young people. Mr. Rohn is correct when he says that children have big hearts.

When Sandy took Rolf to visit the veterans home with a singing group, he gave a resident the two dollars he brought along for a McDonald's burger. Is Rolf a saint? Not on your life, but he has **seen** how fortunate he is and his generosity reflects that belief. Sandy simply provided him with the situation which enabled him to act on his feelings.

Savings and charity. It's important to teach, but all too frequently ignored by all but the top 20% parents who know the absolute value of a consistent, disciplined savings habit and who have experienced first hand the incredible dimension that charity gives to their lives. The only way to experience compassion is to live it, or as close to it as you can get.

When I am asked how much should a child be encouraged to save and give to charity, I answer "I don't know." People in the midwest save more, but the further west you travel the greater the willingness to give to charity. That is also true when you go south. A couple in New Orleans gave me the 80/10/10 rule that seems to agree with most parental goals. 80% of what the child makes can be used as the child wants. 10% goes into savings for the future and 10% is for those less fortunate.

Of all the elements of teaching children the value of money, when it comes to a visual tour to the other side of life, nothing has raised more controversy. It's true, I originally felt the same way. Why disclose life's unhappy side to our young people? Life is tough enough, so let's not complicate it with the fact that life is tougher for others. Let's just go for the happy side and not mention the rest. I mean sunshine is what they need, right?

Well, about two years ago I was flying a trip that spent twenty two hours in New York. What an opportunity. On each trip I would visit some point of interest like the Statue of Liberty or Empire State Building, then go to a Broadway play in the evening. On the third trip I decided to visit the United Nations building. When I got to the east side of Manhattan, I crossed the street to enter the U.N. grounds. There, to my right was a heat grill with a lady sitting on it. I knew what street people were, but here, for the first time, I came face to face with one.

Picture this. I stood there for what must have been fifteen minutes just looking at her. I couldn't take my eyes off her. She was sitting there with three brown bags filled with whatever she treasured and talking to herself. I couldn't understand a word of what she was saying, and she didn't seem to be aware that I was five feet away just staring at her. It was such an intense moment. Looking at her with the U.N. building, and all it stands for, right behind this human being. On the tour, I was told there are 53,000 of these human beings in New York City. That's as many people as live in the city of La Crosse, Wisconsin, where I live. These people could have their own mayor! The tour guide also informed me that they just aren't bums and winos.

Some are people who lost their jobs, lost their middle-class homes in the suburbs, lost everything that we take for granted. She even told me stories of street people with Ph.D.s. Maybe some of these people could use a little compassion.

It's easy to take your son and daughter on a visual tour of the neighborhood fire station and visit your bank. I am convinced it's healthy for parents and kids (teenagers especially) to see the down side of life. Go out of your way to enable your children to experience life's other side. Visit a relative in a nursing home or hospital and hold their hand. I know of a Florida couple who took their boy to a veterans home and visited teenagers who were paralyzed because they weren't wearing their motorcycle helmet. Their son wears his all the time . . . now. Visually visit a poor section of town and remember that this is real.

Teaching kids isn't easy. Teaching teenagers is harder. Talking about teenage pregnancy will give you a headache, and the typical response is, "Oh, Ma!" or "Good grief, Dad, what do you think I am?" A counselor I know says, "Save your frustration and take them for an afternoon to a home for unwed mothers or drug rehabilitation center." It's the emotional impact that gets the message across. Just like my seeing the bag lady. It gets you and you just don't forget. My counselor friend also says that it's very important to assure your young person of your support and love before your visit is over.

Drugs, teen pregnancies, poverty, and mistakes are a fact of life. These visual tours can be hard because it puts us, the parents, in a strange situation that most of us have never confronted. It will, however, add honesty to the parent-child relationship and provide a new dimension to our lives. And that makes it worth the challenge.

"May the force be with you."

....Star Wars

CHAPTER EIGHT

Believing In Magic: "Reality Therapy"

We now have two of the three relatively heavy subjects (savings and charity) behind us. Both are important because they are something that most people do not practice, so each parent must come to grips with these topics before they can be incorporated in successfully teaching children about money. No small task.

Here is where we'll talk about the third heavy, compounding, more completely known as compounding interest. You will, I believe, find this of equal interest to savings and charity. It's important to fully understand compounding because it has a magical effect on our children's, as well as our own, reasons for saving money.

With only twenty out of every one hundred people consistently saving a regular amount of their income, it becomes clear that parents do not have enough reasons to save. Of the twenty who do save, they save a total of 5% of the earning power of this country, as opposed to 30% in countries like Japan where two thirds of the population save consistently.

Why do people save? Answer: for as many reasons as you can imagine. However, a couple of major reasons people save are for their retirement or desire to take life easy **before** they reach retirement age. Some plan savings for a new car or a wardrobe or an important purchase like a home or a long-dreamed-of travel adventure. Kids will save for their education but seldom do it without encouragement from an adult.

To have savings make sense, it is important to understand compound interest. Once that is clearly understood, all it takes is the discipline to stay on path month by month until the goal is reached. Some goals take longer than others, while some arrive sooner than we anticipated.

Discipline is simply doing what we know is best for us, even when we don't feel like doing it — whether that is using our seat belt, brushing our teeth, or saving money. The longer we practice a discipline, the more it becomes a habit. Someone said that if a person maintains a new discipline for just six weeks, it will start to become a habit. By three months it will have become a habit.

One of the strongest motivators for young people to develop a good habit is parental example. If a parent smokes, chances are the child will smoke. If our homes are filled with books and magazines, chances are our children will love reading. If our children see us walking and exercising, chances are they will grow up healthy and fit. If children see mom and dad saving for the future, chances are they will be willing to do the same. So, this section on compounding interest is as much for convincing parents as it is for informing your children. So let's get started.

"Life is a numbers game." 20% of the people in any organization do 80% of the work. Of any group of 100 students, only 5 will be financially independent by age sixty five. And then there is the rule of 72. It says, that when you save money, divide the percent of interest you receive into 72 and that is the length of time it will take for your money to double. That's an important rule to understand. Here is how it works.

Seventy two divided by 3% interest equals 24 years to double your money. That means, if you invested $1000 and receive 3% interest on your money, you would have $2000 in 24 years.

That certainly is not all that impressive. But, understand that, as you save money, the money you save earns interest. As your money earns interest, the interest begins to earn interest and the whole thing begins to compound. That's nice.

More realistically, interest rates are higher than 3% and this is what the rule of 72 will mean:

72 divided by 6% interest = 12 years to double
72 divided by 9% interest =   8 years to double
72 divided by 12% interest =   6 years to double
72 divided by 15% interest = 4.8 years to double
72 divided by 18% interest =   4 years to double

The idea is to get the greatest amount of interest for the money you save. If you will buy this idea, 18% and greater can be possible. But first, let's keep the sell job going and see some of the effects of compounding interest.

Earning interest on interest. Terrific idea! That's what compounding is all about. If you were to put one dollar into a compounding account . . . and understand that I don't believe there is a bank in the world that would let you open an account with only one dollar and just let it sit there like the chart on the next page illustrates . . . but, if you put one dollar into a compounding account at 5% interest, in one year you would have $1.05. That makes sense.

However, in ten years you will not have $1.50, you will have $1.63 because of the compounding effect of interest earned over the past nine years contributing to your total earnings. Now look at what happens to that one dollar when it earns 18% in 50 years. One dollar becomes $3,927.36, thanks to compounding.

ONE DOLLAR EARNING
COMPOUND INTEREST

End of Year	Interest Rate								
	3%	5%	6%	8%	10%	12%	14%	16%	18%
1	1.03	1.05	1.06	1.08	1.10	1.12	1.14	1.16	1.18
5	1.16	1.28	1.34	1.47	1.61	1.76	1.93	2.10	2.29
10	1.34	1.63	1.79	2.16	2.59	3.11	3.71	4.41	5.23
15	1.56	2.08	2.40	3.17	4.18	5.47	7.14	9.27	11.97
20	1.81	2.65	3.21	4.66	6.73	9.65	13.74	19.46	27.39
25	2.09	3.39	4.29	6.85	10.83	17.00	26.46	40.87	62.67
30	2.43	4.32	5.74	10.06	17.45	29.96	50.95	85.85	143.37
35	2.81	5.52	7.69	14.79	28.10	52.80	98.10	180.31	328.00
40	3.26	7.04	10.29	21.72	45.26	93.05	188.88	378.72	750.38
45	3.78	8.99	13.76	31.92	72.89	163.99	363.68	795.44	1716.68
50	4.38	11.47	18.42	46.90	117.39	289.00	700.23	1670.70	3927.36

Eighteen percent for 50 years? Consider this. I am selling you, the parent, on a concept that most parents have never learned to believe in. Our children are the important consideration. With the changes in today's economic conditions, they must learn to appreciate this idea. Eighteen percent is a lot of interest, but a tax deferred annuity or an IRA can produce that kind of interest. As for the 50 years, well, if your fifteen-year-old daughter will buy this idea, she would be 65 in fifty years . . . now it becomes reasonable. This illustration is only meant to show the magic of compounding interest to your teenager, and to their parents.

"Children never listen, but they never fail to imitate." That's what an insightful mother told me in Miami one afternoon. She may be right. If she is, we have to appeal to our children on an emotional level instead of intellectually. The next idea for one's self enlightenment toward the magic of compound interest has been effective with everyone I presented it to. As you tell your child about your goals and what you are doing to make them a reality, get the family checker board out. If you don't have a jar full of pennies, slip on down to your favorite financial institution and get ten or twenty dollars worth.

After a dramatic introduction and explanation of what compounding interest is and a little something about the virtues of saving money for life's eventualities which should include sickness, vacations, and a description of your most recent visual tour through a less fortunate area than the one you now live in, conclude with, "Here now, is the secret of financial security." If your child is under ten, it might be a good idea to have him raise his hand and pledge to keep this secret so that no one else will learn about it because if he does tell, everyone will surely do it and it won't be a secret any longer.

Place one penny on the first square of your checker board. Ask your child or teenager to place two pennies on the second square and four on the third. Double the number of pennies on each square you come to. Your first row will look like this: 1 penny, 2 pennies, 4 pennies, 8 pennies, 16 pennies, 32 pennies, 64 pennies, and 128 pennies.

Look at your pile of pennies next to the checker board and say, "Look at all these pennies I got from our local financial institution today. How many will we have left when we complete the board by doubling the number of pennies on each successive square?"

I have always maintained this would be a great way for parents to plan their children's education fund. One square would be one month. If times are tough, each square could be a year instead. Imagine that! For only pennies a year and a checker board, parents could save for their children's futures. Why don't more people do it, if it's that simple? What really is fantastic is to realize that the financial institution where your money is saved will be paying all the interest. All we have to do is put in a little on a consistent basis.

Look at your huge pile of pennies again (be dramatic) and, if you haven't done this before, realize that there aren't enough pennies known to mankind to complete the board. If you're a chess player, it will take something over a million **dollars** in pennies just to make it **halfway** across the board. In all likelihood, there just isn't enough money on this planet to complete all 64 squares. Hey, doesn't that impress you just a little? I know we are compounding at the rate of 100%, but it sure gets your attention.

To make a point, sometimes we have to get a little extreme. Now raise your hand and say, "I believe in compounding interest." If you will stick with me, I'll take you through a couple more steps and show you results that are as impressive as the checker board . . . and it happens every day.

This idea makes me so excited I can hardly stand it. It's this kind of excitement that will get our children's attention. When we use enthusiasm to get and hold their interest, we have more power than a TV commercial. And our commercial appeal can run for 20 or 30 minutes nonstop when we play our cards (or pennies) right. Emotion with enthusiasm makes every kid listen.

After we saw what happened to one dollar when it is left alone for a while we get an idea what compounding is about. We understand that it isn't practical to put only one dollar aside and leave it there. So, let's take that idea and expand it into some very real examples.

Here is what would happen if your son saved ten dollars a month, but received only 5% compounded interest.

In 10 years he will have $1,560.18
In 20 years he will have $4,132.47
In 30 years he will have $8,373.47
In 40 years he will have $15,365.70

Now, let's reduce the amount of savings by one half and see what happens at several rates of interest. Let's invest (another word for save) only $5 each month. Anyone can come up with $5 each month if they have enough reasons, right? Compounding interest and the rule of 72 are the keys, but a consistent savings habit (time) is what makes the magic.

SAVING $5 EACH MONTH

Years	3%	6%	9%	12%	15%
10	$699	$816	$955	$1,120	$1,315
20	$1,639	$2,279	$3,216	$4,599	$6,635
30	$2,902	$4,898	$8,568	$15,404	$28,159
40	$4,600	$9,589	$21,240	$48,965	$115,234
50	$6,882	$17,989	$51,239	$153,199	$467,502
60	$9,949	$33,034	$122,257	$476,933	$1,892,622

Compounding interest plus a consistent savings program of $5 a month will make you wealthy. A tip for a favorite waitress or a movie once a month costs more than five dollars, but we do this without thinking. The secret is to make savings into the same kind of routine as tipping.

Now you can see that it's not how much you save but, more importantly, the amount of time that you maintain your consistent savings program that makes the difference.

What would happen if, on the day your daughter was born, you had gone down to your favorite bank or credit union and borrowed $1000 (on your signature for repayment over the next couple of years) and put it into an annuity or IRA for your child? Well, if you were in a hurry and asked for only 5% interest here is what you would earn:

In 10 years your daughter will have $1,628.
In 20 years your daughter will have $2,653.
In 30 years your daughter will have $4,321.
In 40 years your daughter will have $7,039.
In 50 years your daughter will have $11,467.
In 60 years your daughter will have $18,679.

OK, that may not seem like much money, and 30 years is a long time. But consider this. As a national average, you (as a parent) do not yet have $4,000 in any savings program. Your goal should be to have that much, and there are some very good reasons why you should.

But, let's see what happens when we don't increase the amount of savings . . . only the compounding interest. If you received 10% on your one-time investment of $1000 this is what you would earn:

In 10 years your daughter will have $2,593.
In 20 years your daughter will have $6,727.
In 30 years your daughter will have $17,449.
In 40 years your daughter will have $45,259.
In 50 years your daughter will have $117,390.
In 60 years your daughter will have $304,481.

The rule of 72 will tell you what the amount will be in 70 years.

"But," you say, "she can't wait until she's 40 to go to college." True. So take this annuity to your friendly banker and give it to him for safe keeping while he provides your daughter with her educational loan. Talk to him on the day you invest your thousand dollars.

"But, daughter of mine, what will you do with the $45,259 when you're 40?" And she says, "maybe I can put my son through college . . . thanks, Dad!"

The possibilities and probabilities are endless. It only takes doing something today to make it happen tomorrow. It's not just the amount you save that counts.

Below is a chart showing what would happen if you saved $1000 as a one-time investment. It uses three different interest rates of 5%, 10%, and 12%. You will see what a difference compound interest (rule of 72) and time will do for your money.

Need money fast? Don't stop the magic. You can always borrow **against** your account and keep the magic.

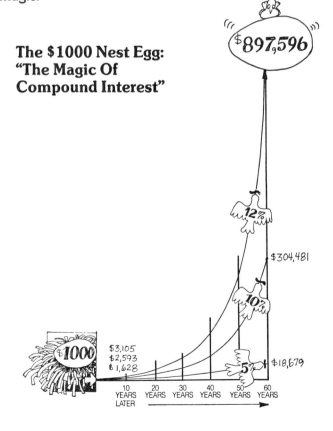

The $1000 Nest Egg: "The Magic Of Compound Interest"

$897,596

12%

$304,481

10%

$3,105
$2,593
$1,628

5%

$18,679

$1000

10 YEARS LATER   20 YEARS   30 YEARS   40 YEARS   50 YEARS   60 YEARS

What would happen if you saved $100 every month instead of just a one-time amount? That is what this illustration is all about. I asked my children what they would do with $92,000 in 20 years. Kari says, "Twenty years! Do you see what I will have in forty years?" Rolf figures he'll get 12% and in 50 years he'll treat his rock band to dinner at McDonald's because he's going to "pull" his money out and "buy" a swimming pool then.

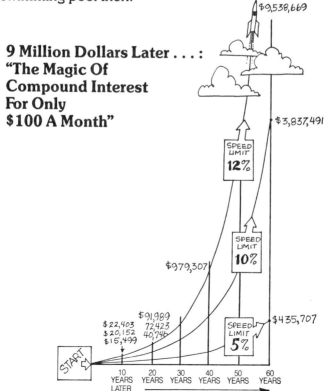

**9 Million Dollars Later . . . :
"The Magic Of
Compound Interest
For Only
$100 A Month"**

$9,538,669

$3,837,491

SPEED
LIMIT
12%

SPEED
LIMIT
10%

$979,307

$91,989
$22,403 72,423
$20,152 40,746
$15,499

SPEED
LIMIT
5%

$435,707

START

| 10 YEARS LATER | 20 YEARS | 30 YEARS | 40 YEARS | 50 YEARS | 60 YEARS |

Today we live in a golden age. This is a time that man has dreamed of and worked toward for thousands of years. Since this is our time, we pretty much take it for granted. In America, we are particularly fortunate because we live in the richest land that ever existed on the face of the earth, a land of abundant opportunity for everyone. But you know what happens? Earl Nightingale is on target in his essay titled "The Strangest Secret In The World." He puts it like this. "Let's take a hundred men who start even at the age of twenty five. Do you have any idea what will happen to those men by the time they are sixty five? These one hundred men who all start even at the age of twenty five all believe they are going to be successful. If you ask any one of these men if he wanted to be a success, he'd tell you he did, and you'd notice that he was eager towards life, that there was a certain sparkle to his eye, an erectness to his carriage, and life seemed like a pretty interesting adventure to him. But, by the time they're sixty five, one will be rich, four will be financially independent, five will still be working. Fifty four will be broke."

Prudential Insurance and the U.S. Department of Health and Human Services say the remaining 36 unaccounted for by Mr. Nightingale will either have died (22) or have an average income of $11,577 per year.

Mr. Nightingale goes on to ask, "Now think a moment. What has happened to the sparkle that was there when they were twenty five? What's become of the dreams, the hopes, the plans, and why is there such a large disparity between what these men intended to do and what they actually accomplished?"

What happened is that too many parents either put off or were never aware that for things to change or get better for them they had to do something. I believe that's why, as parents, we must provide the example to our children. Show the excitement, talk about compounding interest with the checker board, and start believing in the magic. The fact is, if you don't, chances are they never will believe in magic.

"Ready money is Aladdin's Lamp."
....Byron

CHAPTER NINE

Questions And Answers: "Finding Their Hot Buttons"

Throughout this book I have stressed that it may not be possible to take everything I have said as the absolute solution. Life is not that benevolent. Each child is different. I am grateful for that — "I don't know what I would do if I had **their** kid." Use what you can and try what makes sense in your unique situation.

During the four years Sandy and I devoted to preparing this book, apparent contradictions arose and gave way to questions concerning seemingly insurmountable road blocks. Most of these concerns began with a hushed remark like, "well yes, but maybe . . . ." When I hear that, I find a couple of questions are necessary to determine what hasn't worked so far.

The important thing to remember is that we all have uneasy feelings when it comes to deciding what to do next with children and young adults. It's really quite normal. What usually emerges is the realization that we are all plagued with a certain amount of uncertainty — "I am absolutely certain that what I was certain of just might not be so" — because there is always the other side to consider and, like coins, one side is usually as valid as the other.

Having said all that, here are several interesting questions I am most frequently asked.

QUESTION: *"Throughout your talk you have referred to the allowance as unconditional. In your opinion, is there ever a time when the allowance is used as a disciplinary tool?"*

The importance of having an unconditional allowance is to provide a young person with a higher level of self-esteem that can outweigh the monetary value of the allowance. "I belong." "I am part of a family group that accepts me for who I am." "This is my safe harbor." And that is a very important awareness to provide a youngster. However, I do believe there are times when allowances might be used as a disciplinary tool.

A relative of mine stopped his 13-year-old son's allowance when he was suspended from school for a day after being caught with a pack of cigarettes. For some people that's no big deal; but to my cousin, cigarettes are not acceptable.

My view is that a suspension of the allowance should not be the first restriction placed on a young person. Rather, it should be the last. Groundings, privilege revocation, or a low level swat should be used first. The allowance is your child's first encounter with a paycheck experience. Money is a very personal subject in all families. When, however, family values are transgressed, revocation of the allowance becomes a valuable attention getter.

When the allowance is revoked it's much like my daughter training her horse. Kari first makes the horse dependent upon her by restricting him to his stall. She provides him with all the hay, grain, and water he needs. In this situation, her horse becomes much more cooperative in the training ring. Revoking an allowance can do much the same thing with a "fast-forward" type young person.

Nine out of ten parents provide their children with an allowance. Over half of those surveyed monitor how the allowance is spent and forbid spending on certain products or activities (candy, alcohol, R movies, etc. . . . "unacceptable" things). About 40% of the same people attach the allowance to a defined behavior code. These parents believe that since they (the parents) are docked for days missed at work, the children should lose a part or all of their allowance when they fail to live up to parental expectations.

Whichever method you use, the unconditional allowance or the qualified allowance or a combination of both, try to be as consistent as possible.

QUESTION: *"I have one of the 'fast-forward' type children you talk about. His allowance is gone ten minutes after he receives it. His room is a mess, and his sense of responsibility is nowhere in sight. I am so frustrated with him. Any ideas?"*

It's a messy world we live in. Our kids live in that same messy world. For them it's not only messy, but sometimes it just doesn't make any sense. A clue that you're dealing with one of these fast-forward kids is the way they handle their allowance . . . or rather their inability to handle it. I am assured that the bright side to all this is that they are the ones who will make the parent the proudest when they get older. It could be that just leaving home will do the parent proud!

At any rate, a very effective method to use with children that can't control their allowance is the point system. This system is effective with all children and may be considered as a supplement to an allowance. Why it works when the allowance doesn't, I'm not sure. Each time I ask a psychologist, I get the feeling he doesn't know either.

Here is how it works. My cousin, who cut off the allowance for the cigarette episode, took his boy (Mike) for a little visual tour. Understand that Mike is 13 years old, athletic, and smart. He's a nice kid but can drive me to the point of distraction in less than an hour. Yet, he does impress me with his athletic and gymnastic accomplishments.

Where did his dad take him on his visual tour? They spent most of an entire day visiting the recreational vehicle stores in the area. Mike was able to test drive several of the all terrain vehicles (ATV). His dad picked up several brochures and in general got Mike all cranked up over the idea of ATVs. On the way home they stopped for burgers and Mike was approached with the idea of earning his own ATV.

You and I might say that an ATV is dangerous and should not be a part of any family. A piano, a 10-speed bicycle, or maybe a TV set; but an ATV? Never! They should be outlawed.

Be that as it may. The ATV was a hot button that dilated Mike's eyes. Dad had his attention. He met Mike on common ground. As you know by now, the hot button (ATV) is important. Any goal is good but only as long as it is within your means and acceptable to your value system.

Mike's parents developed a chart similar to the one on the next page. They drew a vertical line with 50 point spacings and at each 500 points placed a star for an intermediate goal. A picture of the ATV was cut from a brochure and taped to the top of the chart. On the right side of the vertical point line a list was made of the ways Mike would earn the points along with the point value.

As points were earned, they were drawn with a magic marker. As each 500 point intermediate goal was earned, the item was obtained to keep Mike focused and enthusiastic.

Mike earned his ATV in seven months. In my estimation, the behavior modification his parents sought was a success. Mike has his allowance back, and I, for one, think it was well worth it.

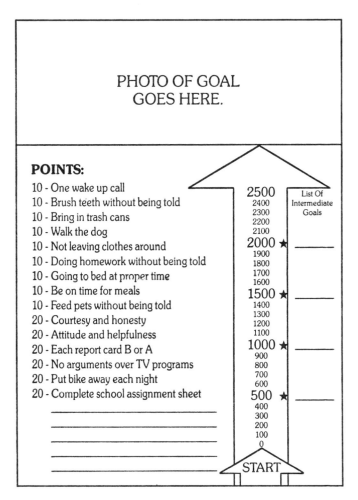

PHOTO OF GOAL
GOES HERE.

POINTS:

10 - One wake up call
10 - Brush teeth without being told
10 - Bring in trash cans
10 - Walk the dog
10 - Not leaving clothes around
10 - Doing homework without being told
10 - Going to bed at proper time
10 - Be on time for meals
10 - Feed pets without being told
20 - Courtesy and honesty
20 - Attitude and helpfulness
20 - Each report card B or A
20 - No arguments over TV programs
20 - Put bike away each night
20 - Complete school assignment sheet

2500
2400
2300
2200
2100
2000 ★ _____
1900
1800
1700
1600
1500 ★ _____
1400
1300
1200
1100
1000 ★ _____
900
800
700
600
500 ★ _____
400
300
200
100
0

List Of
Intermediate
Goals

START

Enlarge on copy machine/adapt points and hang on refrigerator door.

After talking with successful parents who have used the point system, here are some important considerations.

1. Establish measurable goals. They must be as specific and defined as possible. "Keep room clean" is too vague. "100 points for each B on your report card" is measurable and, as a result, free from nagging and conflict.

2. Clearly agree on what must be done to earn points. Kids do try to weasel around things that aren't nailed down. Write down the ground rules and don't change them part way into the program without good reason. That will be taken as the old bait and switch and every kid alive knows how that's played. Don't change the rules. You (the parent) must be reliable, fair, and consistent.

3. Never take points away. Points are earned and should never be taken away once they are earned. To do so will only destroy the incentive.

4. Provide for intermediate goals. It will keep interest high. If the ultimate goal is a long way off, you will maintain interest and encouragement by being there to celebrate the small wins along the way.

5. Deliver on the intermediate and ultimate goal within a reasonable time after it's won. Very important! When they deliver, so must you.

6. Avoid . . . no . . . **never** convert points to money. It's OK to agree on a different intermediate goal. But, never agree to substitute cash.

7. Celebrate the achievement of every goal. Go out for a pizza and focus on the accomplishments. Give your children some positive attention! They'll just eat it up . . . much the same as the average adult. And they'll do what's necessary to get more of that good stuff . . . guaranteed!

8. As much as possible, sample the goal. Let them taste it. Go for a test drive, pick out the color, select the size, talk to experts, and do it several times. Never put it on lay away. That's too much like having earned it already. The possibility of failure must exist.

9. Challenge your kids. Provide an atmosphere where they can be challenged positively, consistent with your values.

10. When extra encouragement is needed, designate the day a "double point day." Award double points for any points earned for one day. Sometimes a pat on the back and a helping hand is necessary. Provide lots of "You can do it" encouragement.

QUESTION: *"What is the single most important lesson to teach a child?"*

When I am asked that question, I am certain I am talking with someone who believes that money could be the root of all evil. I quickly ask them the same question. And they quickly reply (every time) . . . ethics. I realize ethics has a lot to do with learning the value of money, **but** my experience teaches that ethics can't be deliberately taught. What makes you believe your kid will turn out the way **you want**? Ethics are learned through observation. Albert Schweitzer said the greatest role of the parent is to be the example. That's how ethics are taught. I am certain that parental control diminishes as kids get older . . . and then they begin to imitate.

Kids will take attention any way they can get it from their parents. If being good will get attention, they will go for positive attention. If they can get attention only through some negative action, then negative attention is what they will settle for. Attention is attention. In his two great books, *The One Minute Father* and *The One Minute Mother*, Dr. Spencer Johnson talks about the art of catching your kids doing something good. When you catch them doing something good, tell them and let them know how it makes you feel. It only takes a minute and really works wonders.

When parents pay attention to what their kids do right, they emphasize the positive qualities of their kids. This, of course, is not the way most of us were raised. We got caught doing the wrong things. I recommend this whole new approach to behavior. Get a copy of his book and go for it.

QUESTION: *"We have two great kids, they work hard in school and are no trouble at home. However, no matter what we say, they just won't save money. Any ideas?"*

Open your own savings account and be their example. When they see you do it and when you tell them why you are saving, they will be receptive to the idea. That is the solution in 80% of families with your problem.

On the other hand, if you save regularly and have a difficult time getting the message across, here are a few ideas you might look into.

A) Insist. B) Remind. C) Take them to the bank **before** going to the shopping mall.

There are a few incentives you might employ. First, however, plan a time to talk to your children about their goals and the concept of the compounding checker board. Younger children are much more open to the idea of putting money into savings than in their teen years.

Insisting: Parents should insist their young people save a percentage (25% to 50%) of money gifts they receive on special occasions like birthdays, etc.

Remind: It is necessary to remind children (and there is nothing wrong with doing that) they agreed to save a certain percent of their allowance or earnings from extra income opportunities each week.

I like the practice of paying the allowance by check. When the check is cashed at the bank, the savings deposit can be made immediately. This will also familiarize children with the mystery of check-cashing procedures. The temptations created by possessing all available cash and being in the general area of a shopping mall can do terrible things to all but the most determined savings plan.

Matching Savings: Some parents reward their children when they have good report cards. If you do, you might ask, "Before we decide how much you are to receive for these fine grades please tell me what percentage do you intend to put into your long-neglected savings account?"

The idea of matching funds is used much more often than I had expected. One area I found it frequently used is with hobby or clothing purchases. The youngster pays the first half, the parent pays the rest. This way the desire for the name brands is not so expensive for mom and dad. Also, giving allowance only at home (as well as never giving a loan or advance on the allowance) reinforces the savings concept. What would happen if mom and dad asked for a loan or advance against their paychecks?

QUESTION: *"What about adult children moving back home after being gone for several years?"*

Interesting question. Why did they move back? Was it a job loss, divorce, graduation from college, or just the need for a vacation? Just how extended will the stay be? I have heard these reasons and more.

"There's no place like home" and mom and dad's house comes with a couple of bennies you won't find in the outside world — maid service on Saturdays (including washing and ironing), good home cooking, and, in most cases, a banking service for interest-free loans without a repayment plan. And did anyone mention rent?

Any time an adult child returns home for reasons other than a short-term medical recovery, you should examine the alternatives. Anything is better than junior returning with all his earthly belongings and a cute little three-year-old dependent. So long as it's not as comfortable as where he came from he won't outstay your sense of obligation.

Rent should be charged commensurate with services rendered. What would you charge the kid down the street? In your computations include food and other services you provide. OK, discount it if you still feel you have more of an obligation to him than he has to you. Be certain to include some chores to be done around the house that will make your life easier. The unspoken argument that states, "You must be responsible for me (even at age 35) because you brought me into this world" can't hold up today, even for the timid of heart.

No job? No money? Nothing in sight? After two weeks buy him a newspaper with a help wanted section from the nearest large city . . . along with a bus ticket in that direction.

QUESTION: *"At what point in time should the allowance end?"*

There are two times that would indicate it's time to end the allowance. I am assuming we agree that leaving home in the normal progression of life does not include leaving with an ongoing allowance.

The first time is when your child leaves home for school or military service. Now, there is a distinction between an allowance and financial aid. Helping with the cost of school with a check each month is not an allowance because you have specified where the money is to be spent. Hopefully you have specified how the money will be paid back. By doing so, you will provide yourself with the pleasure of whispering, on graduation day, "It's really a gift and not a loan . . . because you have made us so proud on this special day. We love you so much."

Some may continue to call that an allowance, but, for the purpose of this book, it's financial aid for a higher education. It might also be a helping hand while your daughter (now a young adult) is getting established on her own. When that is the case, the money continues to come from you, but it should be designated for a specific purpose, such as rent, or tuition. Without designating its purpose, the helping hand may become an expected second income for many young people. Nice young people, just like yours . . . it can happen.

The other time the allowance should end is when your child is established with a W2 earnings job. This could be McDonald's or some other entry level work experience. However, if the income is limited by too few hours, you may decide to continue to provide a reduced allowance until the work schedule expands to provide the income expected. This would usually be the case while your son is still in school. Once your son is out of school and on his own (while living under your roof) get him off the allowance and onto a checkbook so he can pay rent and see where his money goes. It is important to his growth and self concept to be placed in a responsible position as soon after his school years as possible. Paying rent and services you provide is a big step in that direction.

QUESTION: *"Should a high school or college student be given a credit card?"*

That's a little like asking if a student's grades will suffer if she works while in school. Some will and some won't. As for credit cards, I can see times when it would be a fine idea. Providing a credit card for your student on a study trip to the Orient would make everyone feel better. You can add your child's name to your own bank card for occasions like that. It should go without saying that I would have a heart to heart talk with my student traveler about how **my** credit card will and will not be used. The other consideration is, "How will the charged amount be repaid to the convenient in-house banker?" Remember, the card holder (you) is ultimately responsible for the payment of the charges. This is true regardless of who you have authorized to use your card.

Should your student have her very own charge card? Chances are . . . no. In order for her to have a credit line, you (as parent) will be required to assume responsibility for ultimate repayment. I cannot think of a time when I would jeopardize my own financial status with an **open-ended** commitment like that.

By providing this type of credit you do nothing to help your student establish her credit, since it's your credit you provide through your guaranteed signature.

If your daughter maintains an active savings account (which she opened during her allowance days) and a checking account (with W2 earnings), her bank or credit union will likely be happy to issue her a credit card. That will benefit her more because it's in her name, not yours.

QUESTION: *"From listening to you talk, you seem to have a special relationship with your own children. What advice do you have for parents?"*

Listen to me when it comes to money matters. But, know that I am a total amateur when it comes to raising kids. I have my theories like everyone else and I will share those with you here, as long as you understand that I don't know any more than you about what we are talking about.

I try to follow a couple of rules when interacting with Rolf and Kari. In short this is what they are:

1. Relax, and treat them like I would if they were the kids down the street. That means patience, endless patience. It also means enabling our teenager to understand that we are not the enemy. At the same time that means we make time to listen.

2. Provide structure. Sandy and I **try** to establish reasonable limits as to what is acceptable behavior from them. Kids will test these limits, but they also must have something (established

limits) they can count on. That means loving them when it hurts the most.

3. "You are what you pay attention to." Since I am gone from home for several days at a time, I think it's important to take the time to meet them where they're at — listening to their talk and always trying to get them to say how they feel about whatever is discussed. We try to make a big deal out of their small victories and celebrate special moments. I marvel at the insights I have gotten when I give them my attention.

4. Honesty tempered with tact in all I say to them. It's OK to say no to designer jeans as long as you have an honest reason (cost is an OK objection). They will test your resolve, and when the test is too great for your soul to bear, say so and walk away.

5. We expect respect. We are the adults, we love them, we will listen to them, and it will be done our way. Kari and Rolf both have learned that, with respect, it can be done their way. After all, we are not the enemy.

The problem Sandy and I found with these rules is that they come with a warning. Treat your children this way and things will get better, but (and here's the warning) the process will never end. We wouldn't have it any other way.

QUESTION: *"Not so much a question as it is a request to outline the steps to teaching children the value of money."*

Here are the ten elements of this program as outlined in this book:

1. VISUAL TOURS, filled with emotion, provide the opportunities to relate to the world around us.

2. SHOW AND TELL teaches the mechanics of money.

3. SHORT TALKS help get your values across while still being a friend.

4. THE ALLOWANCE primes the well.

5. FAMILY RESPONSIBILITIES help us realize we depend on each other.

6. EXTRA INCOME OPPORTUNITIES provide a little more control — and the feeling of independence that dawns with realizing you have some control.

7. HOT BUTTONS become real teaching events.

8. SAVINGS make tomorrow's opportunities possible if we start today.

9. CHARITY adds dimension to ourselves — from charity comes purpose.

10. COMPOUNDING is real magic — believe in it.
Good news: Implementation **is** measurable.
Bad news: It never ends.

QUESTION: *"After four years of collecting what unbelievably-little written material exists on the subject of children and money . . . after talking to over a thousand students, singles, parents, grandparents, and some I couldn't identify . . . along with marathon talks with professionals . . . what would I like to add?"*

That's a great question nobody has ever asked! What I would add is this. In today's marvelous age, where technology has given us so many miracles that we begin to take them for granted, there is one thing that I would encourage everyone to do to add a whole dimension to teaching kids the value of money.

If you don't own one, dash out and buy a camera. Everyone take pictures of everything, every celebration of goals won, every pizza eaten, your son on the fire truck, your daughter opening her first savings account, and mom and dad at the picnic by the lake. These are times that go by much too fast. We need a few real memories.

Maybe there isn't time to put your pictures in albums right now, but there will be. Until then, sit around your big box of pictures and remember.

We get a lot of chances to screw up as parents, but in twenty years we can look through our pile of memories and realize that all we had to do was care enough to try to do the right thing and everything worked out pretty well.

"Don't hurry, don't worry. You're only here for a short visit. So be sure to stop and smell the flowers."

....Walter C. Hagen

CHAPTER TEN

Grandparents, Uncles, Aunts . . . :
"One Last Suggestion"

I began this book with the thought that it really is hard being an example for our kids. They are growing up in a world so different from the one we knew at their age. As a result, it's hard for them to understand where we are coming from. Being the example means spending the time focusing on the little things like visual tours, hot buttons, and compounding checker boards.

By now I hope you realize that you can be that example to the extent you are able. We can, and **must**, make that time because it's pretty hard for a ten year old to win when she is in the trench all alone.

Stay one step ahead. That's no small task when you have a fast-forward thirteen year old. But we can if we will always love our children, challenge them, listen to them, and honestly expect something remarkable. They will deliver to the extent they've been taught and we expect.

I would like to be what Rolf and Kari think I am today . . . when they're twenty one. I really think that is what every parent would like.

Whether you're a parent, stepparent, uncle, aunt, big brother or sister, I have a couple of questions for you to think about. "What's your promise?" Don't ask your kids to do what you don't or won't do yourself. And what will they get if they buy it your way?

Your example, your message . . . that's the promise. Examine it. Are you telling your kids that pot is OK at 35 but not at 17? Did you know some parents use X-rated movies as their method of sex education? Can you believe that? It's true!

There is a truth that every child learns about adults one week before being born. It says, "Your actions speak so loudly that I can't hear what you're saying." That signals mom's first contraction. Kids live by that motto from day one.

Some people say love is patience. When it comes to teaching children the value of money, it's true. I am reminded of a very special person I talked with as I prepared this book. She lived in Holmen, Wisconsin. I had the pleasure of visiting with her many times before her death this past December. This particular afternoon, we had coffee and talked about her grand-children and how important it is to teach children the value of money. I asked her what she thought it was all about. After looking out the window a few minutes she quietly said, "Patience, Harold, endless patience. Our children become what we pay attention to."

It's not easy for our kids to make the best possible spending decisions when they are bombarded by commercial appeals, peer group pressure, and adults seemingly out of step with today's synthesized generation.

What about those adults? It's not easy for them either! Another book by Harold Moe, *Make Your Paycheck Last*, "the complete step by step guide to personal and family financial success," was written for them.

Reviewed by *The Wall Street Journal, Changing Times,* and other national publications, plus the Credit Union National Association, "*Make Your Paycheck Last* takes you from where you are and enables you to accurately evaluate your finances, with 'do-able' ideas for fine tuning and improving your financial condition — whatever your situation. More than a financial guide," it includes:

- A complete financial plan, with real examples and explanations of the six major keys to financial security.
- How to set goals that work, with actual examples from real people.
- How to recognize the five financial danger signs, how to avoid being trapped by them, and what to do if you are.
- Seven proven rules for easy credit card control.
- Profitable ways to identify financial problems and turn them into financial successes.
- Checklists . . . guides . . . and much more.

The perfect gift for yourself or anyone trying to get the most from each paycheck! ► ► ►

"Patience, endless patience . . . our children become what we pay attention to."

....Kari Dammen Dodd